SHELLS

A STUDIO BOOK

SHE

Photography by
Text by

LLS

Andreas Feininger
William K. Emerson

THE VIKING PRESS   NEW YORK

This book is dedicated to the billion times a trillion life fragments which through aeons have created an infinite variety of functional forms of marvelous efficiency, breathtaking beauty, and inspirational design.

Text Copyright 1972 in all countries of the International Copyright Union by William K. Emerson
Photographs Copyright 1972 in all countries of the International Copyright Union by Andreas Feininger
All rights reserved
First published in 1972 by The Viking Press, Inc.
625 Madison Avenue, New York, N. Y. 10022
Published simultaneously in Canada by
The Macmillan Company of Canada Limited
SBN 670–63963–x
Library of Congress catalog card number: 72–185874
Line-drawings Howard S. Friedman
Printed in Germany by F. W. Wesel, Baden-Baden

Contents

Acknowledgments

I wish to express my sincere thanks and appreciation for outstanding cooperation by the following organizations, and my great indebtedness to the persons in charge, who graciously lent me shells for photography and trusted me with handling their valuable property:

The Stix Rare Shell Gallery, owned by Hugh and Marguerite Stix,, 13 Vandam Street, New York, New York 10013, specialists in shells of outstanding beauty and perfection for collectors.

The American Museum of Natural History, New York, New York; its Curator of Mollusks and Chairman of the Department of Living Invertebrates, Dr. William K. Emerson; and his assistant, Mr. William E. Old, Jr.

Without their generous cooperation this book would not exist.

A.F.

It is a pleasure to acknowledge the able assistance I received from friends in preparing the text for this book. I am indebted to my colleagues, Mr. William E. Old, Jr., for giving unstintingly of his time and knowledge in furthering the completion of this task, Mr. Morris K. Jacobson for critically reading a draft of the text, and Miss Lynne Judge for undertaking the typing of the manuscript. Mr. Howard S. Friedmann of New York City contributed the excellent line drawings comprising figures 1–7 of the Introduction. Dr. Kenneth J. Boss of Harvard University kindly provided data from his manuscript on the numerical diversity of the Mollusca before his paper was published.

Lastly, I owe my parents an everlasting debt of gratitude for introducing me at an early age to the wonders of nature and for encouraging me to pursue my malacological studies.

W. K. E.

Foreword

This book is neither a guide for shell collectors nor a treatise on malacology, a shell-identification manual nor an attempt to prove that shells are beautiful. Rather it could be called a shell-appreciation book. It is intended as a complement to all the other kinds of shell books.

Because many good shell books of the types mentioned above already exist, producing another one at first seemed to me a waste. However, although most of these shell books fulfill their purpose adequately and occasionally even splendidly, they have one quality in common which, to me, makes them less than entirely satisfactory: they are too much preoccupied with facts. They treat shells strictly from the point of view of the scientist and especially the taxonomist, which, of course, is the only sound *basis* for any shell book, including the present one. But they neglect to open the eye and mind of the reader to the wonder of shells: the infinite variety of structure and form and their relationship to function; the fact that an apparently insignificant lump of slime can produce permanent housings of often breathtaking beauty, daring, originality, exquisite color, and superlative geometrical perfection; the fact that nature has varied the same basic plan in more than fifty thousand different ways, each species marvelously adapted to a particular set of environmental conditions; and the sheer aesthetic pleasure and almost mystic satisfaction one can derive from contemplating these fabulous shapes and designs.

Furthermore, the illustrations of every shell book I know are rather unimaginative and matter-of-fact, showing their subjects more or less as a person would normally see them, thereby adding nothing new to his experience. And while such an approach is, of course, a necessity for quick and reliable identification of shells, it shortchanges the reader by presenting only part of the story. Why? Because there is so much more to be seen, appreciated, and marveled at in any shell than a normal view can reveal. Primarily, because the human eye is an instrument of rather limited capability, inferior in many respects to the more versatile eye of the camera. Not only is the human eye constantly hampered by the fact that it is controlled by a brain encumbered with preconceived ideas, receptive primarily to impressions of immediate interest, prejudiced in regard to manner of subject approach, perception, and rendition, and inherently resisting anything unfamiliar and new, but it also fails to perform satisfactorily if objects are too small to be seen clearly at the closest normal viewing distance of approximately eight inches. In contrast, in the hands of an imaginative photographer respecting no photographic taboos, the camera is free from all these limitations and thus is able to present new and stimulating views of even ordinary subjects.

To be able to take fullest advantage of the camera's inherent potential as an instrument for making discoveries in the realm of vision, I selected my shells and approached them photographically not from the point of view of the scientist but from that of the engineer intrigued by structure and the interdependence of function and form, and from the point of view of the artist who is fascinated by shape and design. The result, I hope, is a new type of shell book – a shell-appreciation book – which, without in any way diminishing the valute of "ordinary" shell books, actually complements these books and enhances their usefulness by making the reader, the shell-collector, and perhaps even the scientist aware of aspects which those other books neglect, showing him things he had not seen and presenting him with viewpoints he had not considered before.

Doubtlessly, some people will say: These photographs are unnatural; this is not the way I see a shell. My reply is: That is exactly what I set out to accomplish when I made my photographs – to show you more or less familiar objects *not* as you are accustomed to seeing them but in a *new* light in order to give you a *new* point of view and provide you with a *new* visual experience. Anybody knows that, fundamentally, "the camera does not lie." Therefore these pictures, all of which are straight and unmanipulated photographs involving neither creative distortion nor special devices or tricks to achieve their effect, cannot be unnatural; they can only be unfamiliar. Who decrees that the familiar way of looking at shells is the only permissible one?

Specifically, I have deliberately violated the academic way of photographing shells in four respects:

1. I have made use of the camera's ability to magnify the subject to any desired degree and have presented most of my shells in an enlarged and sometimes even greatly magnified scale. By this I accomplish two things: I dramatize the familiar – a sure way to capture the viewer's attention. But more important, I am able to show him details of structure, texture, and form which, because of their smallness, he has not seen and appreciated before, thereby adding to his knowledge and visual experience.

2. I have used carefully controlled lighting to bring out significant aspects of structure and design – qualities which in ordinary illumination would have been graphically less effective or lost.

3. I have cropped my pictures tightly, omitting anything in the photograph that I considered superfluous to the desired effect. The result of this kind of graphic condensation is, of course, a heightened emphasis of essential characteristics, greater visual impact, and ultimately a more informative picture.

4. I frequently have used an eye-level instead of the more familiar view of looking down on a shell lying on a horizontal surface. To me, a downward look implies superiority on the part of the viewer – a condescending attitude which does not go with my conviction that all living things are created equal and have equal rights to exist. Besides enabling me to treat shells like works of sculpture – modeling them in all their monumentality – such an eye-level view makes it possible to place them against the sky, thereby bringing into the picture an environmental element implying space and the open sea, which cannot help but intensify the emotional effect of these views. While studying my specimens in preparation for photographing them, I was struck by the fact that many shells possess what might be called "forms of the sea." I was so fascinated by this discovery that I devoted the entire first chapter to pictures of these sea forms, which really express the spirit of this book. There are shells whose spines resemble either a fish-skeleton or the keel and ribs of a wooden hull (plate 1). Some shells bring to mind breaking waves (pl. 2), while others have protuberances which look like flying scud or foam (pls. 4 and 5). Still others suggest soaring sea birds (pl. 3), miniature replicas of a blow-

fish (pl. 6 top), or a marlin (pl. 7); and it is easy to visualize an old-fashioned anchor in the form of the hammer oyster (pl. 6 bottom). Even the most common of all shell configurations, the helix (see chapter V), is a reflection of a whirlpool, a vortex of swirling water.

Though merely coincidental, such similarities between shells and forms connected with the sea not only help to create a mood appropriate to the subject of this book but also stimulate the mind to further investigation regarding the structure and forms of shells. For example – and this is *not* a coincidence – there is the thought-provoking fact that the spines of many shells (see chapter VIII), the purpose of which is doubtlessly defensive, are structurally identical with the defensive spines of certain animals and the thorns of certain plants – a convincing demonstration of the universality of a basic principle in nature.

Another such basic principle is embodied in the fact that corrugating increases the strength of any thin, platelike structure, as exemplified by corrugated cardboard or sheet metal, which is much more resistant to deformation than the same material of the same thickness would be if it were flat. Nature, of course, utilized this principle aeons before it was discovered by man, as is demonstrated by plates 60, 64, 65, 70, and others. If these shells were smooth instead of corrugated, to be equally resistant to damage they would have to be much thicker, a state which would involve the disadvantages of considerably greater expenditure of material plus additional weight.

Corrugation, however, is not the only way of increasing the strength of a platelike structure without considerably increasing its thickness and weight; ribbing will accomplish the same effect. Examples of such ribbed structures are shown in the photographs in plates 86 (bottom left), 91, 95, 129, 134, and 140.

In selecting these and other interesting specimens to photograph from the more than fifty thousand different species of shells, I was fortunate indeed to have two outstanding shell collections at my disposition: that of the American Museum of Natural History and that of the Stix Rare Shell Gallery, both of New York. The Museum's collection, which contains more than a million specimens, is famous for its completeness; the Stix collection is rightly renowned for the outstanding beauty and perfection of its shells. Combined, they enabled me to present the reader with a completely unique selection of the world's most beautiful and interesting shells.

In choosing the shells for display in this book, unlike the authors of most other shell books, I was motivated neither by scientific considerations nor by a desire for completeness (showing at least one representative of each order) but was guided solely by structural and artistic viewpoints. If I found a shell structurally interesting or beautiful in design, I selected it for inclusion in the book; if it struck me as ordinary or dull, I rejected it, no matter how rare or scientifically unique. This, incidentally, is the reason why I don't show a picture of the Glory-of-the-Sea, a rather undistinguished-looking shell which is wrongly represented in most shell books as the rarest, most precious, and, from the viewpoint of the collector, most desirable of all shells.

On Photographing Shells

Contrary to popular opinion, photographing shells is not technically difficult, provided, of course, one uses the right equipment; the real difficulty in obtaining good shell pictures is in the *seeing* – in choosing the right specimen, the most significant angle of view, and the most effective kind of illumination. To answer in advance the many photo-technical questions which shell collectors may want to ask after seeing this book (I cannot answer questions by mail), here is the gist of my own experience as a shell photographer:

I made all my pictures with a view camera because the front and back adjustments characteristic of this kind of camera enable me to get a maximum of sharpness in depth, always a problem in extreme close-up photography. The film size is less important; anything between $2^1/4 \times 2^3/4$ and 4×5 inches will do. Depending on the size of the shell and my intentions, I used one of three lenses: a 13.5-cm Tessar f/6.3, a 168-mm Goerz Dagor f/6.8; or a 24-cm Apo-Tessar f/9. Most of my exposures were made with the diaphragm stopped down to somewhere between f/32 and f/50 for maximum extension of sharpness in depth.

All my black and white pictures were made on Ko-

dak Tri-X film, the color shots on Kodak High-Speed Ektachrome.

The greatest photo-technical problem in shell photography is determining the correct exposure. In close-up photography, the data determined with the exposure meter must always be modified in accordance with the distance between lens and film, which in turn is decided by the distance between the lens and the subject. The shorter the distance from the subject to the lens, the longer the distance between lens and film and consequently the longer the exposure. In the case of a rendition on the film in natural size, the exposure must be four times as long as the value indicated by the exposure meter if the negative or color transparency is to be correctly exposed. A very practical aid in determining the correct exposure of close-ups at different subject distances is the Kodak Effective Aperture Computer, an inexpensive cardboard dial-calculator available at most photo stores.

I photographed some shells outdoors and others indoors. In either case, to avoid multiple sets of shadows, or shadows within shadows, I never used more than a single light source: outdoors, of course, the sun; indoors, a single 500-watt, 3200 K reflector flood lamp used as a boom light, i. e., mounted on a swiveling extension arm attached to the top of a light stand. This kind of arrangement is invaluable because it enables a photographer to swing his lamp into any desired position, including, if necessary, directly above his specimen for overhead light, a form of illumination impossible to achieve if the lamp is mounted in the ordinary way on the light stand. To avoid excessively contrasty negatives and especially color transparencies, I used white cardboard reflectors of various sizes for shadow fill-in.

Naturally, I don't want to imply that excellent shell photographs cannot be made with different equipment. My outfit, for example, would have been totally useless for the production of color slides for projection; in such a case, a 35-mm single-lens reflex camera featuring interchangeable lenses and a built-in through-the-lens exposure meter, in conjunction with an extension bellows, would be the most suitable instrument. On the other hand, certain types of cameras – particularly 35-mm rangefinder cameras (unless equipped with a special reflex housing), twin-lens reflex cameras, ordinary folding and box cameras, and press-type cameras having only single-extension bellows – are basically unsuitable to close-up photography because of parallax problems, insufficient extension between lens and film, or the necessity for special close-up attachments or aids, which are often clumsy or severely restricted in their usefulness.

In arranging the illumination for shell (and other) close-ups, beginners in particular often make the mistake of placing the lamp too close to the specimen in an attempt to shorten the time of exposure by increasing the brightness of the illumination. The price for this saving in exposure time, however, is a negative or color transparency that is unevenly illuminated – overexposed on one side and underexposed on the other, in addition to being too contrasty and, in the end, unnatural appearing. I have found that, for the rendition of a shell of average size in approximately natural size on the film, the distance between the shell and the lamp should be at least twenty-five inches, and preferably greater.

Another common fault of the inexperienced photographer is not to distinguish between lighting for black and white and lighting for color. Actually, for best results in black and white, a raking thirty to forty-five degree side-light is usually the most effective type of illumination because it is the one most likely to render the surface texture of a shell to best advantage through interplay of light and shadow. In color photography, however, this same arrangement, even if supplemented by generous shadow fill-in, is not usually conducive to a natural-appearing color rendition; for color, a more frontally arranged illumination producing less extensive shadows will normally give the best results.

As I have mentioned before, the factor that is most decisive in shell photography and most consequential for the ultimate effect of the picture is the matter of "seeing": What is the best angle from which to photograph a shell? Although this involves, of course, a very personal choice on which no two photographers

(or shell collectors) may agree, one thing is certain: As in sculpture or architectural photography, there will always be instances in which a single view cannot do justice to the beauty or complexity of a specific shell. If this is the case, the only satisfactory solution is to take several shots from different angles, illustrating different aspects of the shell. This, of course, is the reason why, in the following, I sometimes show the same shell in two or more different views. See, for instance, pls. 2 and 133 bottom right; 3 top left, 61 right, and 139; 3 top right and 6 bottom; 4 top and bottom; 6 top and 77; 25 top left and right; 29 and 75; 30 and 74; 66 and 138; 81 and 156 top right; 86 bottom left and 95. I leave it to the ingenuity of the reader to find other examples. In each of these cases, confining myself to only a single view would have meant failing to show an important feature of the shell, and the loss would have been the reader's.

Unlike most other books on shells, this volume, although scientifically accurate down to the last detail, is not organized along scientific lines. Rather, it is the exuberant statement of a naturalist enchanted with the wonder, beauty, and structure of shells. Its primary effect is intended to be visual, appealing to the artist in the reader. To achieve maximum visual impact, I have taken certain artistic liberties, such as combining shells from different localities in the same picture although they would never be found together in reality, or placing a shell that lives on sandy bottoms on a rock to present it better in my photograph. I trust that the reader, no matter whether interested layman, enthusiastic collector, or serious scientist, will forgive me for such "inaccuracies," which I deliberately employed in the interest of maximum aesthetic effect, and that he will get as much enjoyment out of contemplating the resulting photographs as I got out of making them.

Lillinonah, May 1972   Andreas Feininger

Introduction

Shells:
Their Form and Function in Nature

Long before the dawn of civilization, man was an avid shell collector. Mollusks were first used by man as food, and their shells are to be found in the garbage heaps – kitchen middens, as archaeologists call them – that mark the oldest-known human occupational sites. Anthropologists have interpreted the presence of nonendemic species of shells found in association with primitive human remains as indicating the existence of trade routes over considerable geographical distances. The earliest known collections of trade shells date from Cro-Magnon man, some 25,000 years ago. Artifacts recovered from caves inhabited by Cro-Magnon man in France include tropical seashells that do not live in European waters. Exotic species from these sites, including the Red Helmet snail, suggest trading activities existed between primitive Europeans and residents of the Indian and Pacific Oceans. Trade shells from the tropics also have been found throughout the Ancient World at cultural sites which predate the construction of the great Egyptian pyramids by many centuries. Ancient occupational sites in the New World likewise have yielded trade shells.

In classical times, Aristotle contributed scholarly discourses on mollusks, and he most likely possessed a large reference collection of shells from the Old World. His accounts of molluscan biology, dating from 336 B.C., provide the beginning for modern malacological and conchological research.

Conchology, known as "la belle science" during the Victorian era, is the branch of zoology which embraces the systematic arrangement and description of mollusks based largely upon a study of the shell. *Malacology*, on the other hand, is the study of the entire molluscan animal, the soft parts as well as the shell. This chapter serves to introduce the layman to the biology of mollusks and thereby to provide the reader with a better understanding of the modern science of malacology. Thus informed, the novice can gain an appreciation of the evolutionary processes that have produced, through aeons, the multitude of wondrous forms and functional diversity exhibited by molluscan shells.

What Is a Mollusk?

Mollusks form one of the largest and most diverse groups of the invertebrates, or animals without backbones. Of the slightly more than one million species of animals known to inhabit our earth, the invertebrates constitute nearly ninety-five per cent, of which the insects are by far the largest group with some 850,000 known species. Mollusks, second only to the insects in the number of species, are classified in the phylum Mollusca, one of the twenty-seven major divisions of the animal kingdom. The number of living species of mollusks was recently estimated to be approximately 50,000. Perhaps less than twenty per cent of the marine mollusks are still unknown to science and most of these await discovery in the ocean depths. In addition to the extant molluscan species, approximately 55,000 extinct species have thus far been described from fossil deposits of the six continents.

To the zoologist, the various kinds of mollusks are not difficult to recognize. The layman associates these invertebrates with the familiar edible shellfish such as oysters, scallops, clams, and snails, and with the many other kinds of shelled mollusks that are better known to the shell collector. This definition is too narrow, however, as it excludes the shell-less groups such as the slugs and octopuses, and those with vestigial internal shells such as the cuttlefish. Other invertebrates have external shells or tests that may be confused with the molluscan shell. These include the bivalved brachiopods, called lamp shells; the echinoderms, including sand dollars, sea urchins, and starfish; and the crustaceans, exemplified by the crabs, lobsters, and shrimps. Their shells, however, are of a different origin, and these animals are not classified with the mollusks. Shellfish, of course, are not fish, which are vertebrates; the term shellfish is restricted in use to the shelled invertebrates, especially the edible mollusks and crustaceans.

Certain mollusks are of major economic importance,

some beneficial and others harmful to mankind. As we've already suggested, of course, a good many species are commonly consumed by humans. The shells of fresh-water clams are cut into buttons, or they may be used in the form of beads to seed artificially cultured pearls. Pearls, whether natural or cultured, together with other mollusks, are used for jewelry and for other forms of personal adornment. Many land snails and slugs are agricultural pests and some fresh-water snails serve as intermediate hosts for parasites that transmit serious diseases to man and his domesticated animals. Furthermore, mollusks, both in larval and adult stages, form an important part of the food chains that support higher animals living on land or in aquatic environments.

Because of their great diversity of form and function, there is no stereotype molluscan form, but there is a basic uniform pattern, the result of their common ancestral origin. As their name, derived from the Latin word *mollis*, meaning soft, implies, the mollusks have a soft body with a slippery skin, and most possess an exoskeleton that forms a hard, limy, external shell. The molluscan body, with the exception of one small class, is unsegmented and consists typically of an anterior head, a ventral foot, and a dorsal visceral mass. A thin fleshy mantle more or less surrounds the body and it is commonly sheltered within the protective shell.

Before we describe the various classes that compose the phylum, it is desirable to discuss briefly the anatomical features that characterize the mollusks, for it is the soft-bodied animal that produces the exoskeleton. And it is this skeleton, the shell, that we value for its beauty and for its appeal to our natural curiosity. The body is enclosed in a thin, capelike mantle that secretes a limy shell of one, two, or eight parts. As we have said, however, in some groups the shell may be greatly reduced in size compared to the body, may be internal, or may be completely lacking. The snails and squids have well-developed eyes and tentacles and a well-formed oral cavity. The clams, oysters, and other bivalves lack a structured head or cephalic region. Situated between the thin mantle and the visceral mass is the mantle cavity, into which the gills and the ducts of the intestines and kidneys empty their waste products. Inside the oral cavity, or mouth, is a ribbonlike set of chitinous teeth, the radula — a dental structure unique to the mollusks.

The teeth serve to grasp tiny food particles; they vary in number and size. A radula typical of the moon snails is shown in the accompanying figure. The radula is not present in the bivalves, which eat small particles of organic matter by trapping them in mucous strands formed in the mantle cavity or by removing the food particles after ingesting sand and mud.

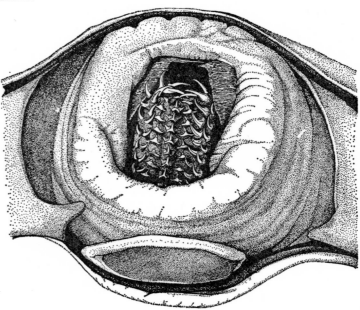

The oral region of a moon snail (*Natica*), showing the radula extended in the open mouth. (After H. Colton, 1908.)

Contained in the visceral mass are the internal organs of circulation, respiration, digestion, and reproduction. The dorsal heart commonly has two chambers and circulates colorless or bluish blood. The excretory tubes of the generally paired kidneys open into the mantle cavity. The digestive tract, often U-shaped or coiled, starts at the mouth, continues through the stomach, follows through the long intestine, and also terminates in the mantle cavity. The sexes are commonly separate, although both sex organs may be present in an individual, as hermaphrodism is not uncommon in several of the classes. The fertilized egg may develop into a tiny multiciliate, trochophore larval stage that is free-swimming and is followed by a more advanced larval stage, called the veliger, which is present in most mollusks. In some species, the larval mollusk is retained in the egg capsule until it matures to a miniature form of the parent and it then crawls or swims out of the capsule. The ventrally placed, muscular foot is variously modified for crawling, burrowing, or swimming.

The Major Groups of Living Mollusks

Figure 1. The phylum Mollusca is divided into seven classes represented by soft-bodied animals exhibiting widely differing degrees of adaptive specialization for aquatic and terrestrial life.

I. Class Aplacophora
Solenogasters are wormlike marine mollusks lacking a shell but with the exterior body covered with shelly spicules.

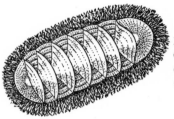

II. Class Polyplacophora
Chitons are limpetlike marine mollusks with eight overlapping shelly plates joined to each other by a fleshy girdle.

III. Class Monoplacophora
Gastroverms are cap-shaped marine mollusks with internal organs and gills paired and arranged in separate groupings.

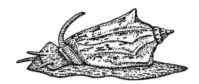

IV. Class Gastropoda
Snails or univalves are marine, fresh-water, or land inhabitants, commonly with a coiled, single shell, or rarely shell-less.

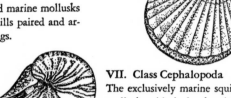

V. Class Scaphopoda
Tusk or tooth shells are marine dwellers with curved, tubular shells open at both ends.

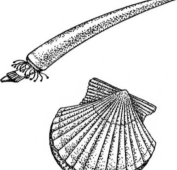

VI. Class Bivalvia (Pelecypoda)
Bivalves—the clams, oysters, and scallops—are marine and fresh-water mollusks with two valves joined by a hinge, a horny ligament, and one or two muscles.

VII. Class Cephalopoda
The exclusively marine squids, octopuses, and nautilus are mollusks with the head region provided with tentacles, large eyes, and powerful jaws. Shell is commonly lacking or internal, rarely external.

The Classification of Mollusks

The phylum is divided into seven major groups, called classes. These divisions are based largely on important anatomical differences of the shell, head, and foot and the respiratory, reproductive, and nervous systems. The classes reflect the wide differences of specialization induced by evolutionary processes within the phylum – see figure 1, above. All seven of the classes are represented by marine species, but only the gastropods and bivalves have adapted to live in fresh water, and only the gastropods are land dwellers. The size of the classes varies greatly, from five living species known in the case of the monoplacophorans to nearly 38,000 species of extant gastropods, which constitute about three-quarters of the living mollusks. The clams and their kin are the second largest group, followed in order of size by the cephalopods, chitons, scaphopods, solenogasters, and monoplacophorans. Approximately half of the mollusks live in the oceans; the others are terrestrial or live in fresh water.

In addition to the seven classes described here, there are a few extinct groups of mollusklike fossils that have been afforded the status of classes in the phylum by paleontologists.

I. Class Aplacophora

The aplacophorans (meaning "non-plate-bearers"), which are commonly known as solenogasters (meaning "channel-stomach," referring to the median longitudinal groove on the ventral surface), form a small group of bilaterally symmetrical, wormlike mollusks (figure 1). These strange creatures lack a head, mantle, foot, shell, or kidneys. They possess a cuticle provided with calcareous spicules and a straight digestive tract; the slitlike mouth is commonly provided with a radula. Most are hermaphroditic. The uncoiled body of these elongate, vermiform mollusks is covered with one to several layers of limy spicules. In most of the species the spicules are minute and the spiculose, skinlike integument appears to be smooth, imparting a sheen to the body.

Most species are small, less than an inch long, but a few are known to attain a length of six inches or more. Because of their small size and the fact that the species must be collected largely by dredging, solenogasters are poorly known. All are marine. They are world-wide in distribution, and they have been recorded from depths ranging from a few feet to the abyssal zone. Only about 250 species have been described. Some live in mud or other soft substrates, forming their own burrows by crawling into the sea bottom. More commonly they are found coiled around other organisms such as soft corals, on which they feed.

Solenogasters were at one time classified with the chitons, with which they share many primitive molluscan characters. It is now believed that solenogasters are not retrograded or secondarily simplified chitons. They apparently represent an early group that evolved independently of the chitons from a common ancestor. They have remained in a more primitive state than the chitons, which have progressed further along the typical molluscan lines. Owing to the lack of a shell, the remains of these animals have not been recognized in the fossil record.

II. Class Polyplacophora

The polyplacophorans (meaning "many-plate-bearers") have an elongate, limpetlike body bearing a shell composed of eight overlapping calcareous valves, or plates (figure 1). The members of this group are better known as chitons, a name derived from the Greek word for the outer shirtlike garment worn by men in classical times. Because of the armorlike plates, these mollusks are also called coat-of-mail shells.

The uncoiled dorsoventrally flattened body is bilaterally symmetrical with a small anterior head lacking cephalic eyes and tentacles, a mouth provided with a radula, a coiled intestine, and a terminal anus. The eight limy plates commonly overlap and are joined to each other marginally, or rarely entirely, by a thick, fleshy girdle, which may be ornamented by scales, bristles, or spines. The mantle, of which the girdle is a part, covers the dorsal and lateral surfaces of the body, and the long, broad foot occupies most of the ventral surface. The gills, numbering from six to eighty in different species, occur in a marginal groove

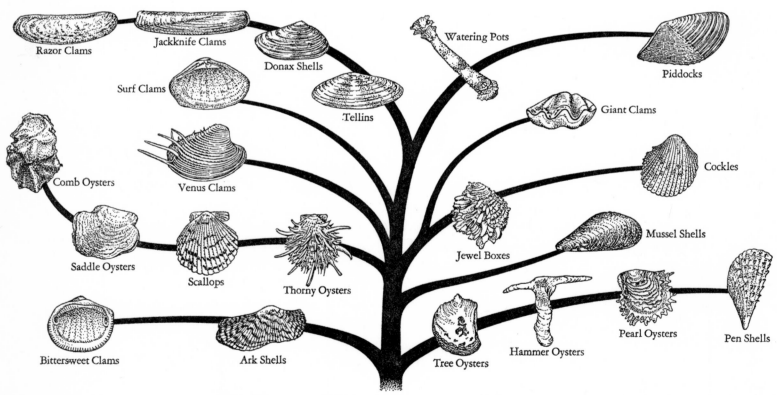

Major Groups of Living Marine Bivalves in Synoptic Series

Figure 2. Examples of the bivalves (pelecypods) are illustrated in hypothetical phyletic succession. Additional information on the classification of these mollusks is presented in the Catalog of Marine Shells at the end of the book.

bordering the flat foot and the mantle. The heart lies posteriorly, in a dorsally placed cavity from which the excretory organs drain. The nervous system lacks a cerebral ganglion, or nerve center in the head region. The sexes are separate; some species brood their young. The large dorsally placed gonad opens into the marginal groove. Fertilization is external. Some species have light-sensitive spots in the skinlike integument covering the plates.

These marine animals adhere to rocks or other hard substrates, from the tidal zone to the oceanic depths. They crawl slowly on their foot and, when disturbed by predators, clamp tightly down on the foot. If dislodged, they curl up into a ball, much as an armadillo does when it is disturbed. They are largely nocturnal feeders, and the radula is used to scrape algae and micro-organisms from the rocks. Some have a homing instinct, returning after browsing to their domiciliary site.

This small class is represented by approximately 600 living species. These range in size from tiny forms, less than a quarter of an inch long, to one species that attains nearly a foot in length. This ancient group, the least altered of the living mollusks, appears early in the fossil record. About 350 fossil species have been described, dating from the Cambrian Period.

The failure of these primitive mollusks to adapt to less restricted habitats is reflected by the relatively small number of living species. Although they are poorly preserved in the fossil record, the chitons appear to have always been a minor group of the molluscan clan.

III. Class Monoplacophora

The monoplacophorans (meaning "single-plate-carriers"), which also have been termed gastroverms ("stomach-worms"), are represented by many extinct species of fossilized univalve shells that superficially resemble limpets, small cap-shaped snails. The class was thought to have become extinct in late Paleozoic time – some 280 million years ago – until a "living fossil" was dredged recently in very deep water off the west coast of Central America. Subsequently, four additional species were discovered in the abyssal depths: a second species in the eastern Pacific

Ocean, one off the Hawaiian Islands, one in the western Atlantic Ocean, and one in the western Indian Ocean.

The finding of living representatives of these primitive mollusks, named *Neopilina* ("new-cap"), in 1957 caused considerable excitement among biologists, who at first believed they had discovered the "missing link" between the wormlike molluscan ancestor and the true mollusk, for the anatomy of the gastroverm was found to have paired organs. This condition was interpreted by some scientists as being homologous to that found in the annelid worms, which are segmented. Most malacologists now concede that the pairing of the organs in these rare mollusks is secondary; that is, the present species evolved from individuals that had a single set of organs.

The *Neopilina* are characterized by the small cap-shaped shell, with a body having an anterior mouth and a posterior anus, the muscles and other internal organs and the gills paired and each arranged in a sequence of five or six individual pairings. A radula is present in the mouth; eyes and tentacles are lacking. The interior of a living specimen is depicted in figure 1.

IV. Class Gastropoda

The gastropods (meaning "stomach-footed") include the familiar land snails and slugs, the marine snails such as conchs, whelks, limpets, and a multitude of others, together with the fresh-water snails. The conspicuous anterior head and the ventral, elongate foot exhibit bilateral symmetry; but the visceral anatomy is typically contained in a dorsal shell (figure 1), and the visceral mass and shell become coiled in the embryonic stages and thus are asymmetrical. The unchambered shell, if present, is one piece and is known as a univalve.

The earliest gastropods presumably had bilateral symmetry throughout. In the course of evolution, however, the digestive tract, anus, heart, kidneys, and many of the nerve ganglia of the living species have been rotated 180 degrees, and some structures have become rudimentary or have been completely lost as a result of this peculiar twisting. This unique growth phenomenon, termed torsion, takes place

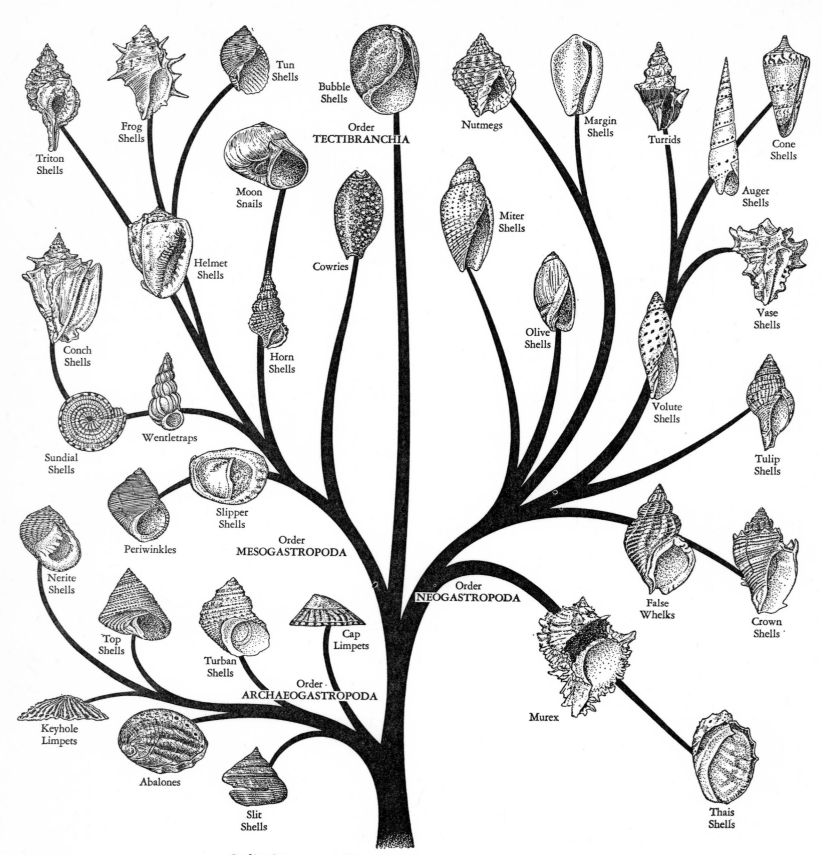

Ordinal Groups of Living Marine Snails in Synoptic Series

Figure 3. Examples of important families of shelled gastropods are pictured to show a hypothetical phyletic succession. The families are discussed and other species are illustrated in the Catalog of Marine Shells at the end of this book.

The Anatomy of Gastropods (Univalves)

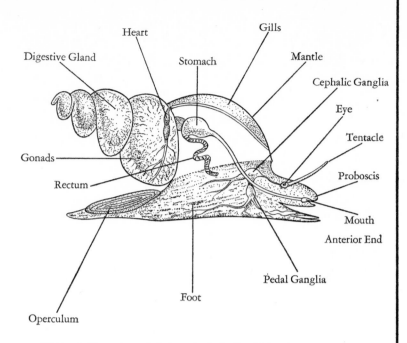

Figure 4. The gastropods have a single shell, which is here removed to expose the gross internal anatomy. Most gastropods are shelled and have a well developed head with paired eyes and tentacles and a large foot adapted for crawling. Feeding is aided by a chitinous radula in the mouth. The mantle secretes the shell and may produce an operculum.

The Anatomy of Bivalves (Pelecypods)

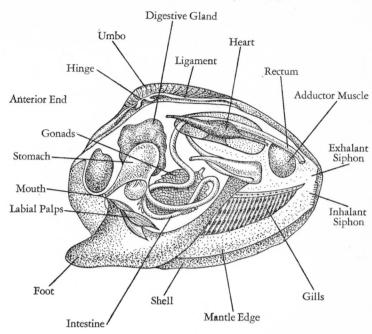

Figure 5. The bivalves—including oysters, scallops, and clams—have two shelly valves, hinged at the top, and commonly possess a hatchet-like foot adapted for burrowing. A head and radula are lacking; feeding is aided by the gills. The mantle is modified posteriorly into tubular siphons which draw and expel water from the mantle cavity.

early in the embryological development of the larval snail. The bilaterally symmetrical larva twists so that all the organs behind the neck region are reversed in position and the mantle cavity moves up and forward over the head. The displacement of the mantle and shell from the enclosed visceral mass occurs during successive growth stages, accompanied by the cessation of development of one half of many of the paired organs, including the heart, gills, and kidneys. As a result of the rotational process, the asymmetrical and spirally coiled body is a flat or an extended helix. The gross anatomy of a gastropod is illustrated in figure 4.

The fossil record suggests that the coiling of the gastropod shell evolved before torsion. The spiraling of the shell and torsion, therefore, reflect separate evolutionary events. The pretorsion shell is believed to have been bilaterally symmetrical with a plano-spiral shell (not conical spiral) having each spiral situated completely outside of the one preceding it and in the same plane, much like a rope coiled flat on the deck of a ship. These planospiral shells eventually

evolved asymmetrical coiling in which the coils were laid down around a central axis, called the columel-la, with each coil formed beneath the preceding coil. In this way these mollusks evolved the compact, distally expanding coiled tube that forms the cone-like shell that is typical of most modern gastropods (figure 1). Not all existing gastropods, however, have asymmetrical shells, and some symmetrical shells have been secondarily derived through retro-gressive evolutionary processes. These qualifications also hold for torsion. The bodies of some gastro-pods apparently have retained the original unaltered symmetry and are termed untorted, while others have more or less undone torsion and are called detorted, following the terminology of my respected colleague and mentor, the late Libbie H. Hyman.

Most gastropods have a single coiled or cap-shaped shell; a few lack shells completely, such as the adult nudibranchs; some have greatly reduced or vestigial shells, which may be internally placed, as in the body of the sea hares. A very few gastropods have two shells, and these exceptional snails resemble bivalves.

A radula, tentacles, and a pair of eyes, together with a horny or limy operculum attached to the back of the foot, are common anatomical features of the gastropods. These structures, as we have seen, may be lacking in some species.

The gastropods exhibit an infinite variety in the shell and soft anatomy (figures 3 and 6). The shell may be elongate or flattened, conical, toplike, spindle-shaped, or cylindrical; the surface of the shell may be plain or highly ornamented with ridges, spines, and other structures. The shell may be white or variously colored, often with a high luster. Most gastropods can withdraw their bodies completely into their shells, and they may have a protective plate, the operculum, to cover the opening, or aperture, of their shell. In some species the operculum is greatly reduced in size, or may be lacking. In the absence of an operculum, land snails secrete a temporary covering of mucus and lime, termed the epiphragm, to cover the aperture of the shell. The gastropod shell commonly is coiled clockwise as seen from the spire, the top of the specimen. These shells are termed right-handed, or dextral; left-handed or sinistral marine snails are rare.

The soft body of the snail is attached to the central axis of the protective shell, termed the columella, from which it can only partially extend from the apertural opening. Most gastropods have a well-defined, bilaterally symmetrical head, which is provided with tentacles and eyes and terminates with the mouth. The ventral surface of the body serves as the foot, which is modified in various ways for locomotion, including crawling and swimming. The mantle is a collarlike fold of the body wall providing a space in the body whorl, the mantle cavity, which is situated between the mantle and the extendable parts of the body mass. The mantle may be extended into a spout, the siphon, to occupy the siphonal canal of the shell and function in respiration. The mantle cavity typically contains the respiratory organs (gills or lungs) and the terminal outlets of the excretory and reproductive systems. The spirally coiled visceral mass is located in the larger turns of the body above the head and foot. This mass of organs commonly includes most of the digestive system, the heart, the nephridium, which serves as an excretory organ, the "liver," and the greater part of the reproductive system (see figure 4). In gastro-

pods lacking shells, such as the nudibranchs and land slugs, the visceral mass and the foot form a single undelineated body.

The digestive tract is composed of the muscular pharynx, the stomach, and the intestine and terminates in an anal orifice. The ducts of the salivary glands empty into the pharynx, whereas the stomach receives the ducts of the large "liver," more precisely termed the midgut gland. The chitinous radula, when present, projects into the floor of the pharynx and consists of a basal membrane bearing numerous rows of teeth.

The common gastropod respiratory organ is the gill. Gills are lacking in land and some fresh-water snails, being replaced by a pulmonary sac, which serves the function of a lung. Respiration in nudibranchs is achieved in plumelike extensions of the dorsal surface, the branchia.

The heart, enclosed in a pericardial cavity, is provided with one ventricle and one or two auricles. Blood vessels enter and leave the heart, but most circulation is completed through open sinuses of the body. In contrast to the more primitive solenogasters and chitons, the nervous system of the gastropods is provided with definite ganglia that are largely concentrated in a ring near the pharynx.

The class Gastropoda, totaling approximately 37,500 living species, is divided into three subclasses and these are further subdivided into orders. The largely aquatic subclass Prosobranchia, with gills commonly placed anterior to the heart in the mantle cavity, are the most numerous and are dioecious; that is, the sexes are separate. Some are herbivorous, including the limpets, top shells, and turban snails, which form the order of primitive marine gastropods, the Archeogastropoda, which have one or two gills and a radula with numerous rows of teeth. The others are omnivorous marine and fresh-water species, and they are placed either in the order Mesogastropoda – the conchs, strombs, cowries, etc. – or in the order Neogastropoda, which includes the murex shells, volutes, and cones, the distinction being based largely on differences in radular morphology. The Mesogastropoda and the Neogastropoda are assigned by some malacologists to a single order, Caenogastropoda, because of the presence of only one set of comblike gills and a radula with no more than seven teeth per row. The subclass Opisthobranchia, with gills placed posterior to the heart, are marine snails, which commonly have a reduced or internal shell, such as in the bubble snails and sea hares, respectively, or lack a shell, as in the nudibranchs. These hermaphrodites are mostly herbivorous, although some are parasitic and lack a radula. The subclass Pulmonata, made up primarily of the land snails and slugs but including some fresh-water and marine snails, have a modified "lung" and are hermaphrodites that feed largely on vegetation. The major groups of marine gastropods are illustrated in phylogenetic order in figure 3.

The gastropods, together with the bivalves, are richly preserved in the fossil record, both classes dating from the Cambrian Period.

V. Class Scaphopoda

The scaphopods (meaning "boat-footed" or "digger-footed") form a distinctive class of marine mollusks that have an unchambered, tubelike shell that superficially resembles a diminutive elephant tusk or, in some species, a tiny canine tooth of a carnivore. Thus the common names, tusk and tooth shells, are applied respectively to these mollusks. The calcareous tube, which is open at both ends, is slightly to moderately curved and is narrowed posteriorly (figure 1). The tube is commonly sculptured with longitudinal or annular ribs; in rare cases it lacks surface ornamentation. The body closely fits the shell, to which it is attached on the dorsal side by muscles.

The characteristics of the muscular foot serve to distinguish the two families of the class. In the tusk shells, the family Dentaliidae, the foot is pointed, with a fleshy collar interrupted dorsally to give a trifid appearance. In the tooth shells, the family Siphonodentaliidae, the foot is provided with a terminal crenulated disk. A head is lacking, the mouth being situated in a projection of the pharynx; a simple but strong radula with five teeth in each row is present. Eyes are not developed, but tassels, termed captacula, composed of many prehensile filamentous tentacles which terminate in tiny food-gathering, clublike capsules, arise at the base of the snout. The mouth opens into a V-shaped intestine, the posterior part of which contains a stomachlike organ into which the ducts of the liver open. The intestine forms several loops and terminates in the posterior

anal opening near the visceral ganglion. The rudimentary heart lacks auricles. The primitive circulatory system consists of five major sinuses. Respiration occurs by an exchange of gases through the wall of the mantle. The well-developed nervous system is typically molluscan. The paired excretory organs open into the mantle cavity below the retractor muscles. Sexes are separate and the sexual products are discharged through the right excretory organ. Fertilization is external.

These marine animals are largely restricted to subtidal waters; some species occur in the oceanic depths. The shell is held in an oblique position in silty to sandy substrates, with the foot extended out of the larger opening of the tube into the bottom sediments. The posterior third of the tube is exposed above the surface of the bottom to permit the circulation of water. The expanded contractile tentacles catch minute organisms such as Foraminifera from the surface of the substrate as the animal burrows into the sediment.

About 350 living species are known, ranging in size from those an eighth of an inch long to a few attaining a length of five inches. Geologically, the scaphopods are an ancient group, dating from the Ordovician Period, but representatives of the class are not commonly found in the fossil record until late in the Mesozoic Era. Approximately 400 fossil species have been described, mostly from the Tertiary Period.

VI. Class Bivalvia

The bivalves (meaning "two-valves") include the clams, oysters, scallops, and mussels. These uncoiled animals are bilaterally symmetrical and laterally compressed, with the soft body enclosed in a shell of two lateral valves, which are hinged together middorsally and are attached by a ligament at the top (figure 1). The membranous mantle is bilobed. They lack a head, pharynx, jaws, radula, or tentacles. The muscular foot is wedge-shaped, giving rise to another name for the bivalves: pelecypods (meaning "hatchet-footed"). A third name for this class, lamellibranchs (meaning "plate-gills"), refers to the nature of the gills, which are thin and platelike. The internal gross anatomy of a bivalve is illustrated in figure 5.

The bivalves, which constitute the second largest

class of mollusks, have successfully adapted to aquatic environments; lacking lungs, they are not land dwellers. About two-thirds of the 7500 living species are inhabitants of salt water, while the others live in fresh-water ponds, lakes, streams, and rivers. Most species burrow in sand or mud by using the muscular foot; some attach to solid objects by byssal threads or limy cement; and a few, such as the scallops, swim by opening and closing the two valves. The active scallops have evolved numerous eyes along the margin of the mantle, which serve as light receptors to detect movement or shadows. The eyes are of a low functional level, being unable to define shapes.

The two valves form a rigid exoskeleton that protects the soft body and provides for attachment of the muscles and hinge ligaments. The right and left valves may vary considerably in size or shape, and they commonly possess, in the dorsal region, several internal hinge teeth, which align the valves with each other and serve as a pivot when the clam opens and closes the shell. Adductor muscles and the dorsally placed, elastic hinge ligament hold the valves in place. The oldest part of each valve, called the beak or umbo, is usually located above the hinge. The morphological features of the bivalve shell are shown in figure 7.

The shell is increased in area by additions of lime secreted by the mantle and deposited around the outer margins of the valves and in thickness by successive deposits of nacre, the porcellaneous inner layer, called mother-of-pearl if it is iridescent. The concentric lines on the outer surface of the valves indicate intervals between successive growth periods. These lines may represent seasonal growth lines in some species living in cool or cold waters, or in the case of those inhabiting tropical waters, growth may occur throughout the year until the individuals attain maturity.

The soft body (figure 5) is made up largely of the median visceral mass, which is enclosed in the shell and comprises various organs; the lower part forms the muscular foot. The paired gills occur on either side of the visceral mass and are covered by the mantle lobe. The mantle adheres marginally to the

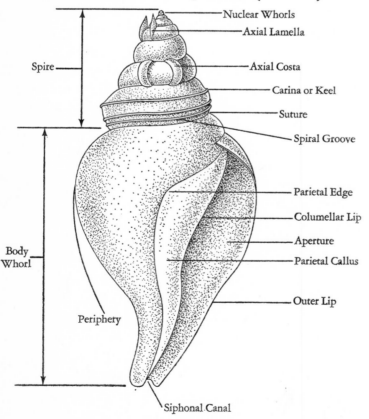

Figure 6. **Composite Figure Illustrating the Parts of a Gastropod Shell (Univalve)**

Nuclear Whorls
Axial Lamella
Axial Costa
Carina or Keel
Suture
Spiral Groove
Parietal Edge
Columellar Lip
Aperture
Parietal Callus
Outer Lip
Siphonal Canal
Spire
Body Whorl
Periphery

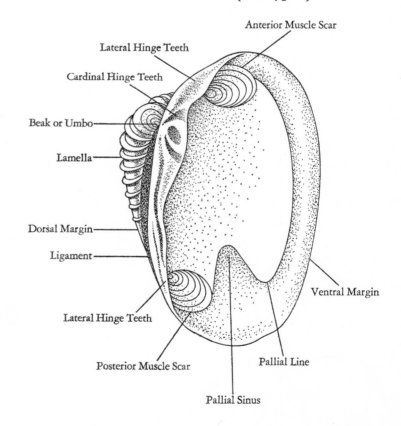

Figure 7. **Composite Figure Illustrating the Parts of a Bivalve Shell (Pelecypod)**

Anterior Muscle Scar
Lateral Hinge Teeth
Cardinal Hinge Teeth
Beak or Umbo
Lamella
Dorsal Margin
Ligament
Lateral Hinge Teeth
Posterior Muscle Scar
Pallial Sinus
Pallial Line
Ventral Margin

inner surface of each valve along the pallial line, a thin scar marking the attachment to the shell of the marginal muscles of the mantle. The muscular edges of the mantle close together to form the mantle cavity. The mantle typically terminates at the margins posteriorly to form two openings, the ventral or incurrent siphon and the dorsal or excurrent siphon. These tubes are fused in some species and are lacking in others. Water containing food particles and waste products circulates in and out of the siphons by the action of tiny cilia that line the surface within the mantle cavity.

Prominent scars on the inner surface of each valve indicate the areas of attachment of the muscles. The large transverse anterior and posterior adductor muscles draw the valves closed; in some species, such as the highly specialized scallops and oysters, only one adductor muscle is present. Other muscles serve to retract and protract the foot into and out of the shell.

The digestive system consists of a small, mouthlike opening behind the foot and between the fleshy labial palps, a short esophagus, a small stomach connected by ducts with the paired digestive glands, and a dorsally placed rectum, with the anus opening into the excurrent siphon. The intestine commonly has a flexible rod, the crystalline style, which produces enzymes useful in digesting starchy substances in the food such as tiny planktonic organisms.

The nervous system includes three pairs of ganglia, one near the esophagus, one in the foot, and one in the viscera.

The circulatory system includes a heart, major blood vessels including a posterior and anterior aorta, and a series of blood sinuses. Blood may be oxygenated in the mantle as well as in the gills. There are four major types of gills, and the class has been divided into orders on the basis of the structure of these respiratory organs, together with certain characters of the shell hinges. The most primitive order, the Protobranchia, have gills that are flat and platelike. In the order Filibranchia, including arks, mussels, oysters, and scallops, the gills are long and bent backwards. In the cockles and clams, order Eulamellibranchia, the gills are united by cross-channels to provide greater space for the exchange of gases. In the dipper clams, order Septibranchia, the gills are reduced to slits in the wall of the respiratory chamber. The

major groups of marine bivalves are illustrated in phylogenetic sequence in figure 2.

In most species, the sexes are separate; a few are hermaphroditic. Some oysters exhibit protandry; that is, the female phase is replaced by a male phase, and these phases may later be reversed again. Fertilization is usually external. The gonads discharge the ova and sperm directly into the surrounding water. The larval young are free-swimming for a period of time before settling to the bottom. Fresh-water mussels have a specialized larva, called glochidia. These larvae must attach to the skin or gills of fishes before developing into young mussels. Some bivalves protect their eggs in brood pouches until the young develop into miniature forms of the adults.

VII. Class Cephalopoda

The cephalopods (meaning "head-footed") have attained the most advanced degree of structural complexity among the mollusks. All are capable of rapid locomotion by means of jet propulsion. The living forms of these exclusively marine animals have largely lost an external shell through the process of evolution. Although shelled forms are common in the fossil record, most of these species became extinct, as did all the dinosaurs, by the end of the Cretaceous Period, some 70 million years ago. Only one family, represented by the Chambered Nautilus (figure 1), has survived with an external shell, which is divided into numerous gas-filled, pearl-lined chambers. Some modern groups do have an internal shell. An internal shell is lacking, however, in all the octopuses and some of the squids. If there is an internal shell, it may consist of a chalky "bone" in the sepioid cuttlefish, or a thin, flattened, rodlike support, the "pen," in certain squids, or a chambered, coiled shell, recalling a tiny ram's horn, in the *Spirula* squids. These reduced or vestigial shells are embedded in the dorsal mantle within the body cavity. The female *Argonauta* secretes a parchmentlike "shell," actually a receptacle to hold the eggs, from which it receives the common name Paper Nautilus.

These externally bilaterally symmetrical animals have a well-developed head with large eyes of advanced perfection, powerful parrotlike, chitinous beaks, and a strong radula within the pharynx. The foot is modified into a set of arms which encircle the mouth and possess suckers, except in the nautiloids; two to four gills are present; the heart has two to four auricles, and the circulatory system is largely contained in blood vessels. The sexes are separate. In some species, the male uses a modified arm, called the hectocotylus, to transfer sperm to the female, which at maturity may reach a much larger size than that attained by the male.

The living representatives of these predacious carnivores are allocated to two subclasses, largely on the basis of the arrangement and number of tentacles present. The subclass Tetrabranchia includes the genus *Nautilus*. The subclass Dibranchia consists of three orders, the Decapoda for the cuttlefish, the Vampyromorpha for certain deep-sea, octopuslike forms, and the Octopoda for the true octopuses.

Many forms are capable of producing clouds of ink and of changing color rapidly. Luminescent organs occur in certain deep-sea species. And the giant squids take the honors of being the largest of invertebrates. The estimated 600 living species of cephalopods represent the zenith of evolution among the molluscan clan.

I.
Forms of the Sea

The oceans cover nearly three-quarters of the surface of the earth at the present time. From the primeval seas, the birthplace of organic life, man has inherited a vast and diversified array of animals and plants. The profuse flora and fauna of the oceans have long held the interest of man in his search for the answers to the perplexing secrets of the natural world. Among the most fascinating of the marine denizens are shells. Although primitive man used mollusks for food and their shells for utensils, trumpets, money, and personal adornment, shells eventually became objects for man's attachment as cult and religious symbols, and as the subjects for art and sorcery.

As evidenced by their role in the history of mankind, shells have long evoked in man an aesthetic appreciation of the infinite variety of form and structure exhibited by these lovely creatures. The artistic beauty displayed in the world of mollusks is dramatically portrayed in the pictures selected to illustrate this chapter and those that follow.

In this introductory chapter are seen majestic forms depicting the intricate senses of nature. The delicate spines of the Venus Comb Murex (pl. 1) give elegance and strength to an otherwise frail shell. The spray of the splashing surf is recalled by the multifrond spines of the Japanese Murex (pl. 4) and the Endive Murex (pl. 5). The motion of the sea is suggested by the form of the coarsely sculptured Open-mouthed Purple (pl. 2), which is a snail shell with the appearance of a clam shell. The paired valves of the Winged Tree-Oyster (pl. 3 top left), the Common Hammer Oyster (pl. 3 top right), and the Distorted Hammer Oyster (pl. 3 bottom) suggest a bird in flight. The Grinning Tun (pl. 6 top) and Martini's Tibia (pl. 7), gastropods with distinctive architectural designs, serve to contrast bulk and simplicity on the one hand with fragility and splendor on the other, and to invite ichthyological comparison: the former suggests a beached blowfish, while the latter, with its long, tibialike siphonal canal, is reminiscent of a spearfish. The Common Hammer Oyster (pl. 6 bottom) makes us think of the forked anchors used by sailing ships of yesterday.

Listed below are the English vernacular names of the shells shown in the plates of this chapter, with reference numbers (which also appear on the plates) to the "Catalog of Marine Shells" that follows chapter IX, where the reader will find a brief description of each species and a picture of the shell reproduced in natural size. This same format is used in each of the following eight chapters.

1.   Venus Comb Murex (13–2)
2.   Open-mouthed Purple (13–42)
3 top left.   Winged Tree-Oyster (23–1)
3 top right.   Common Hammer Oyster (23–2)
3 bottom.   Distorted Hammer Oyster (23–3)
4.   Japanese Murex (13–14)
5.   Endive Murex (13–13)
6 top.   Grinning Tun (12–10)
6 bottom.   Common Hammer Oyster (23–2)
7.   Martini's Tibia (9–10)

I
Murex triremis Perry (13–2) ▶

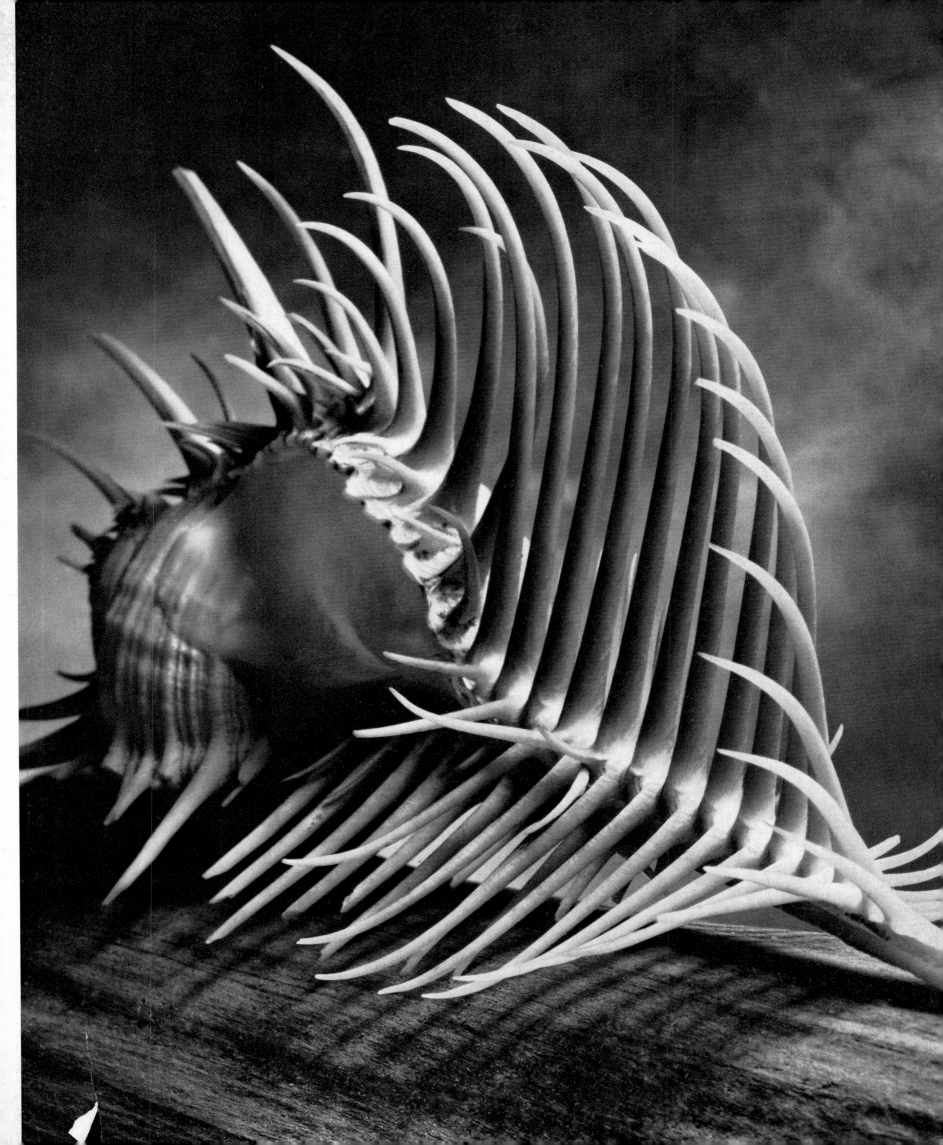

2
▲ *Concholepas concholepas* Bruguière (13–42)

3 top left
Isognomon isognomon Linné (23–1) ▶

3 top right
Malleus malleus Linné (23–2) ▶

3 bottom
Malleus normalis Lamarck (23–3) ▶

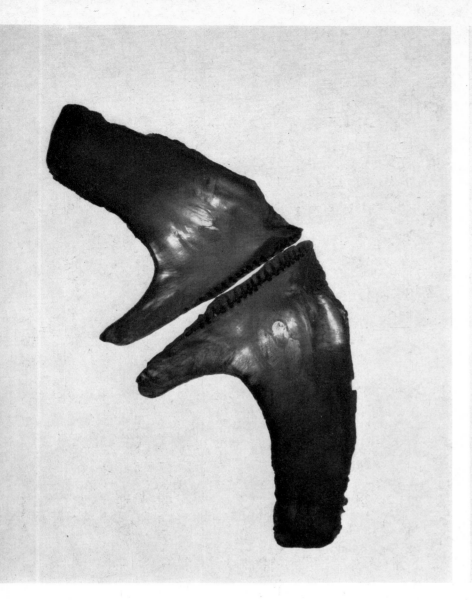

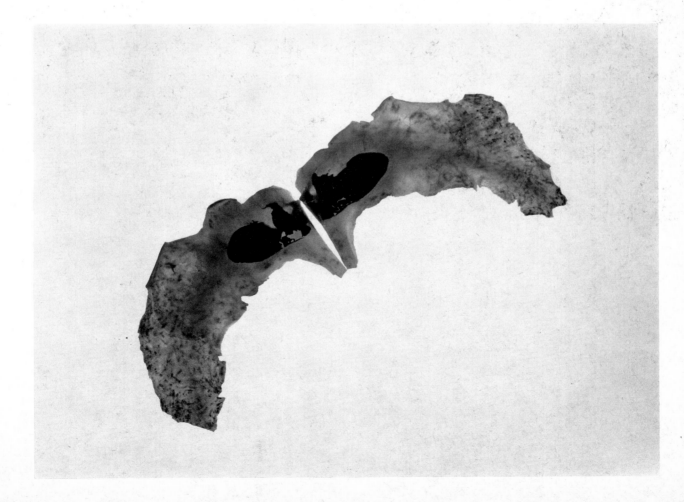

4 top and bottom
Chicoreus asianus Kuroda
(13–14)

5
Hexaplex cichoreus Gmelin (13–13)

6 top
Malea ringens Swainson
(12–10)

6 bottom
Malleus malleus Linné (23–2)

7 top and bottom
Tibia martinii Marrat
(9–10)

II.
An Infinite Variety of Shapes

The wide variety of shapes and forms displayed by the molluscan shell is the result of the adaptive nature of these creatures. Most mollusks are slow moving and are restricted to rather specialized habitats. Thus limited, they have adapted evolutionally since they first appeared in the fossil record in early Cambrian time – some 600 million years ago – into several major groups of dissimilar-looking creatures. Their success as a phylum reflects their ability to adapt to major changes in the natural environment by altering the outlines of their body as new structures were required in order to survive in the various ecological niches available to them in the sea, in fresh water, and on land. Therefore, this plastic group of invertebrate animals reflects the evolutionary stamp of the environment in more obvious ways than those of groups of animals possessing greater powers of locomotion.

The first mollusks probably lacked hard shells, and they inhabited the oceans. The soft-bodied mollusks eventually developed limy shells, and they subsequently also adapted to life in brackish water, in fresh water, and on land. At the present they live in a great variety of substrates – mud, sand, gravel, rocks – in aquatic environments as well as on land. Mollusks have been successful in adapting to all habitats, from the splash zone of the beach to the abysses of the sea, and from the shore to the mountaintop, in forests, deserts, marshlands, and caves, and even underground. They have penetrated all bodies of fresh water, from the brackish estuaries to inland streams, rivers, and lakes. Some mollusks are external or internal parasites and live on the "life blood" of other species of mollusks or other kinds of invertebrates.

But most mollusks are not parasitic. They are free living, and they feed on such different kinds of food as terrestrial and marine plants, living and dead, land and marine animals, and even on man-made objects, such as wooden wharves and ships. Some are able to drill holes in or burrow into hard substrates, including shells, corals, rocks, and logs, and even penetrate the lead cables of submarine telephone lines.

They move slowly by crawling, swimming, or floating, and, less commonly but more rapidly, by jet propulsion as in the case of the squid and its close relatives. The only mode of locomotion that the mollusks have not achieved is the ability to fly through the air, although some squids are able to skim over the surface of the water for a short distance. Land snails, however, are known to crawl to the tops of tall trees and even occur near the summits of high mountains.

Mollusks are found living in all the marine and terrestrial climatic zones, the largest variety of species being found in the tropical seas and the lush tropical jungles. They are also well represented in temperate seas and land areas; the number of species is reduced, but the fewer species are represented by larger populations than those found in the tropics. In the polar regions even fewer species occur, but many individuals of the same species may be present.

Mollusks range in size from the giant squids, attaining some sixty feet in length, and the giant clams, weighing more than five hundred pounds, to minute clams and snails which, when fully grown, are no larger than the head of a pin and would require several thousand specimens to fill a tailor's thimble. The largest living chiton, Steller's Chiton, attains a length of about ten inches, but most species are much smaller. Vernede's Tooth Shell, the largest living scaphopod, reaches nearly five inches in length, which is small compared to some extinct species that are nearly a foot in length.

Faunal Distribution

Zoogeographically, the mollusks found living in the shallow waters of the seas are divided into several major faunal provinces, each of which is characterized by a fauna possessing a high degree of endemic species. The richest areas are those represented by the tropical oceans in which four great faunal regions may be identified. These are the Indo-West Pacific, the Eastern Pacific, the Western Atlantic, and the Eastern Atlantic, which, in turn, are divided into re-

◀ *Angaria melanacantha* Reeve (3–9)

gional faunal provinces (see map p. 234). The boundaries of the provinces are restricted by physical and oceanographic barriers which serve to limit the kinds of species that can live in each region. The tropics, for example, are bounded to the north and south by the 20° C. isotherm for the coldest month in the year. This temperature regime roughly corresponds to the limits of tolerance for the growth of coral reefs. The tropical faunas are further separated longitudinally from each other by land and hydroclimatic barriers that also serve to restrict the faunal composition of each region.

The Indo-Pacific Province, the largest and richest of the faunal regions, extends from the shores of east Africa eastward through the Indian Ocean and into the western Pacific Ocean to Polynesia, northward to southern Japan and the Hawaiian Islands and southward to include the Great Barrier Reef of Australia. These tropical waters are characterized by well-developed coral reefs and a unique assemblage of mollusks such as the giant clams (pl. 46), scorpion conchs (pl. 23), tibia shells (pl. 30 right center and bottom), and heart cockles (pl. 41). The Indo-West Pacific and eastern Pacific areas are separated by the East Pacific Barrier, a vast expanse of deep water that lies between Polynesia and the west American shores. Only a few species with long-living larval stages, or those with adult forms that can attach to floating objects or to swimming organisms, have successfully migrated westward across this water barrier. As a result, the Indo-Pacific Province and the tropical Panamic Province, which extends from the Gulf of California, Mexico, to northern Peru, each support distinctive faunas at the species level.

The New World Land Barrier, with the Isthmus of Panama forming a narrow connection between Central and South America, serves to bar the migration of marine life between the tropical eastern Pacific and the western Atlantic Oceans. As recently as three million years ago, however, the two regions were connected by seaways, with the result that the Panamic Province and tropical Caribbean Province, which centers in the West Indies and extends north to the Florida Keys and Bermuda and south to northern Brazil, have some species in common and many "twin" or closely related species. The composition of the Panamic Province differs largely from that of the Caribbean Province in the paucity of species living in association with coral reefs, which are poorly developed in the tropical eastern Pacific Ocean. The West American Panamic fauna is especially rich in species living on sand and rocky bottoms and supports an abundant and colorful molluscan fauna. The present Panama Canal has not significantly altered the relationship of these faunas, because the canal passes through bodies of fresh water, which form an effective barrier to most marine species. The construction of the proposed sea-level canal across this land barrier, however, could provide a means for marine animals to migrate freely in either direction. It has been predicted by some conservationists that an exchange of faunal elements would cause a large-scale extinction of species in the eastern Pacific as a result of the competitive dominance of species from the western Atlantic. In order to prevent such irrevocable changes in these faunas, means should be developed to prevent the exchange of species through the proposed canal.

A broad expanse of deep water, termed the Mid-Atlantic Barrier, separates the western Atlantic tropics from the tropical coastal waters of West Africa. It is apparently less effective as a barrier to migration than the corresponding deep-water mass in the central-eastern Pacific Ocean. Many species of marine animals, including fishes and invertebrates, occur on both sides of the Atlantic basin in the tropical regions. The majority of such trans-Atlantic species, however, seem to have originated in the western Atlantic and then migrated eastward.

8.   Tarantula Dolphin Shell (3–9)
9.   Turk's Cap (3–22)
10.   Black Murex (13–25)
11.   Winged Murex (13–28)
12 left.   Crenulate Auger (16–38)
12 left center.   Subulate Auger (16–36)
12 right center.   Triseriate Auger (16–39)
12 right.   Crispa Turrid (16–1)
13 left.   Kaderly's Turrid (16–4)
13 center.   Southern Turrid (16–5)
13 right.   Babylon Turrid (16–2)
14.   Imperial Star Shell (3–16)
15.   File Fig Shell (12–12)

9
Turbo sarmaticus Linné (3–22) ▶

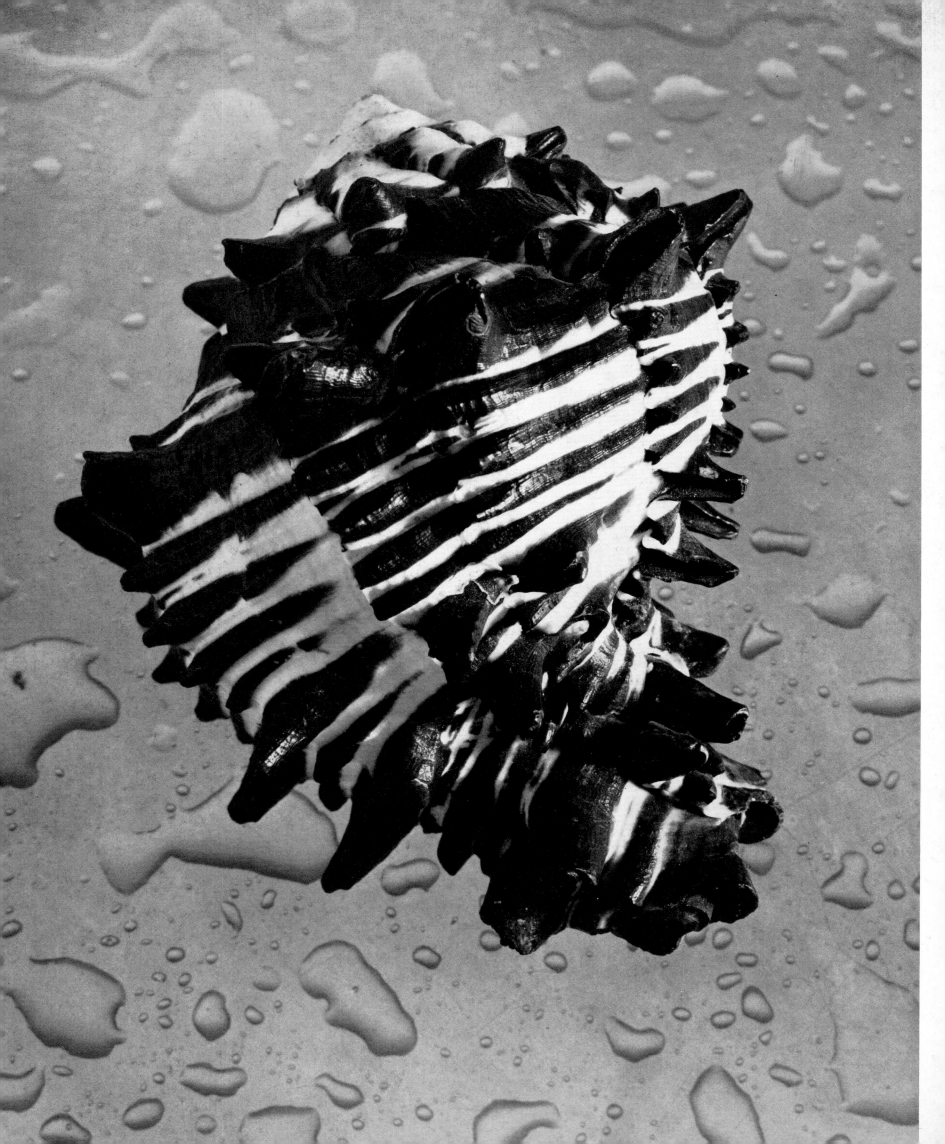

10
◀ *Muricanthus nigritus* Philippi (13–25)

11
Ocinebrellus eurypteron Reeve (13–28) ▲

12 left to right
Terebra crenulata Linné (16–38)   *Terebra triseriata* Gray (16–39)

Terebra subulata Linné (16–36)   *Turris crispa* Lamarck (16–1)

13 left to right
Comitas kaderlyi Lischke (16–4)

Turris babylonia Linné (16–2)

Nihonia australis Roissy (16–5)

14
Guildfordia yoka Jousseaume (3–16) ▲

15
Ficus filosus Sowerby (12–12) ▶

Furthermore, the limited number of species that have migrated westward probably originated in the tropical Indo-West Pacific region and then gained access to the eastern Atlantic by rounding the Cape of Good Hope. A few species that apparently originated in the eastern Atlantic seem to have been successful in becoming established in the western side of the Atlantic Ocean. Some groups, such as the harp shells (pl. 136), became extinct in the Caribbean Province, but representatives survived in the eastern Atlantic and the eastern Pacific, as well as in the Indo-West Pacific region. Representatives of other groups, for example the Grinning Tun Shell (pl. 6 top), are known to occur only in the fossil record of the Caribbean region, and now are to be found living only on the northern Brazilian coast in the Atlantic Basin, but have survived in the tropical eastern Pacific.

The Old World Land Barrier separates the East Atlantic and the Indo-West Pacific regions. Presumably this land barrier has existed at least since the beginning of the Pleistocene, more than a million years ago. The Suez Canal has served as a man-made sea-level passage between Eurasia and Africa since it was opened in 1869. Migration of marine animals has been inhibited, however, by two natural barriers. Part of the Suez passageway includes the highly saline Bitter Lakes, and the canal connects two zoogeographic regions separated by a temperature barrier, the tropical Red Sea and the warm-temperate Mediterranean Sea. Despite these natural barriers to migration, some species have moved through the Suez Canal into the eastern Mediterranean and are apparently replacing rather than coexisting with certain species that are native to the region.

In studying the distribution of the tropical marine faunas, we must conclude that the Indo-West Pacific region serves as the evolutionary and distributional center for the tropical shore animals of the world. Although a few shallow-water species are circumtropical in distribution, it appears that only competitive dominant species have been able to migrate from the rich Indo-Pacific faunal Province eastward across the open ocean to west America and westward around the Cape of Good Hope into the eastern Atlantic. Since the opening of the Suez Canal in 1896, others have been able to pass northward by means of the Canal into the eastern Mediterranean.

Many provincial names have been applied to the marine faunas occurring in the temperate, boreal, and polar regions of the continents and insular land masses. These provinces are intended to represent regions of the shallow coastal waters which have at least fifty per cent of the species peculiar to each faunal province. Only the major provinces are well defined, being separated by land barriers and by critical changes in the hydroclimate.

Some species migrate into adjoining provinces and others are widely dispersed in deep water, or are wide-ranging pelagic species that may occur throughout an ocean basin. These cannot be assigned to any faunal province.

The most isolated of the temperate faunas is the Mediterranean Province, including the Black Sea, Madeira, the Azores, the Canaries, and the northwest coast of Africa to the Bay of Biscay.

In North America temperate waters support faunas of the Californian Province along the West Coast from Point Conception, California, to Cedros Island, Baja California, Mexico, and the Carolinian Province on the East Coast from Cape Cod, Massachusetts, to the northern half of Florida and westward into Texas. The warmer waters of the southern parts of these provinces support some colorful shells, but most of the species have drab, cool-water characteristics.

To the north of the Californian Province are the cool-water Oregonian Province and the cold-water Aleutian Province, which includes the coasts of Alaska to British Columbia, Canada, the Aleutian Islands, and the Sea of Okhotsk. The Carolinian Province is bordered to the north by the cool-water Boreal Province, which ranges from Cape Cod to the Gulf of Saint Lawrence and includes the south coast of Iceland, Norway, the Shetlands, the Faroes, the British Isles, and the Baltic Sea.

The cold waters of the Arctic Province extend above the Arctic Circle, the east coast of Kamchatka, the southern end of Greenland, and along the east coast of Canada down to the Gulf of Saint Lawrence. The relatively few species represented in this province are mostly somber in appearance; many of these species also occur in the Boreal Province.

Corresponding temperate, boreal, and polar provinces are represented in the Southern Hemisphere. In the Western Hemisphere, the Peruvian and Pata-

◀ *Cellana exarata* Nuttall (2–2)

gonian Provinces are warm-temperate, and the Magellanic Province, which includes Tierra del Fuego and the Falkland Islands, is anti-boreal, or southern boreal. The Antarctic Province, including the adjacent islands in the southern ocean, is cold-water. In the Eastern Hemisphere, the isolated South African and the Australian Provinces are cool-water regions that contain rich faunas for these southern areas. The faunas of the New Zealandic Province encompass both the warm-temperate and anti-boreal zones. The Japonic Province, including the east coast of Korea and the islands of central Japan, is situated between the cold-water Aleutian Province and the tropical Indo-Pacific Province. It contains a distinct fauna of warm-temperate forms. The southern Japanese islands are richly endowed with sub-tropical and tropical elements of the Indo-Pacific fauna and various kinds of slit shells, cowries, cones, and volutes occur there.

Number of Species

The phylum Mollusca is commonly spoken of in the literature as including an estimated 80,000 to 100,000 species, placing it as a group second only to the insects in the number of extant species inhabiting our earth. Recent estimates of the number of living molluscan species vary from a high of approximately 107,000 species to a low of about 42,000 species. These widely divergent estimates result from different methods used in compiling data from the information in the literature. The maximum figure includes all the scientific names employed for the described species. We know, however, that many species have been named several times: *Anadonta cygnea* Linné, a fresh-water mussel of Europe, for example, has been given more than five hundred specific names! Many species have received more than ten scientific names, and most species have at least one synonym.

In the most recent survey on this subject, based on a detailed study of the literature, there were calculated to be, on the average, four names available for each living species of gastropod and bivalve known to science. Taking into consideration this excessive naming of species, it was estimated that there are approximately 35,000 species of mollusks known. Allow-

ing for possible errors in compilation and for the number of species yet to be discovered, it was concluded there are nearly 47,000 living molluscan species. These may be allocated to the seven molluscan classes as follows:

1. Aplacophora (solenogasters), 250 species
2. Polyplacophora (chitons), 600 species
3. Monoplacophora (gastroverms), 10 species
4. Gastropoda (snails, etc.), 37,500 species
5. Scaphopoda (tooth shells), 350 species
6. Bivalvia (clams, etc.), 7500 species
7. Cephalopoda (octopuses, squids, etc.), 600 species.

A conservative estimate based on our present knowledge, therefore, suggests that there are about 47,000 to 50,000 species of living mollusks. About 55,000 additional species of extinct mollusks have thus far been described from the fossil record.

The gastropods are the most common group of mollusks, representing three quarters of the living species. The second largest group are the bivalves. In this chapter are pictured some of the more interesting shells of marine gastropods and bivalves to demonstrate how these mollusks have evolved shells with a variety of shapes and forms for life in the diverse habitats of the marine environment.

Most of the species depicted here inhabit shallow water near the shore on mud, sand, gravel, coral, or rocky substrates. Many are exposed by low tides and

16. Hawaiian Limpet (2–2)
17. Heliotrope Star Shell (3–13)
18 top. Rooster Conch (9–12)
18 bottom. Violet Spider (9–22)
19 top. Pilsbry's Spider (9–20)
19 bottom. Burnt Murex (13–20)
20 left. Elongate Spider (9–23)
20 right front. Diana's Ear (9–14)
20 right rear. Lavender Conch (9–13)
21 left front. Gem Triton (12–8)
21 rear. Iredale's Conch (9–15)
21 right front. Dove Conch (9–16)
22. Triumphant Star Shell (3–15)
23. Scorpion Shell (9–24)

18
Strombus gallus Linné
(9–12)

18
Lambis violacea Swainson
(9–22)

19
Lambis crocata pilsbryi
Abbott (9–20)

19
Chicoreus brunneus Link
(13–20)

20 left
Lambis digitata Perry (9–23)

20 right front
Strombus aurisdianae Linné (9–14)

20 rear
Strombus sinuatus Lightfoot (9–13)

21 rear
Strombus vomer iredalei Abbott (9–15)

21 left front
Cymatium rubeculum Linné (12–8)

21 right front
Strombus plicatus columba Lamarck (9–16)

22
Guildfordia triumphans Philippi (3–15) ▲

23
Lambis scorpius Linné (9–24) ▶

are active only at night, when they venture forth from their domicile to feed. Some species, such as the fragile star shells (pls. 14, 22), occur only in deep water, below the photosynthetic zone, where they are adapted to the severe water pressure of the depths.

Although the ultra-abyssal faunas are not well known, living specimens of bottom-dwelling mollusks have been dredged in submarine trenches more than six miles beneath the surface of the sea. The bathymetric record for mollusks is held by a species of clam which was obtained at a depth of 10,687 meters (35,053 feet) in the Tonga Trench. The following are the known maximum depth records for the other molluscan groups: gastropods, 9530 meters; chitons, 9403 meters; and scaphopods, 7657 meters. Only a few species, however, are thought to live in these extreme depths.

Shell Form and Life Habits

Limpets (pl. 16) live on rocky shores, attached to the rocks by means of a remarkably strong muscular foot which enables them to maintain their place despite the action of waves and currents. The large foot fills the opening of the cap-shaped shell of these snails. The paper-thin Fig Shell (pl. 15) is supported by an expansive, fleshy foot that seemingly is larger than the aperture of the shell. The true conch shells (pls. 18 top, 20 right front and rear, 21 rear and right front) and the spider conchs (pls. 18 bottom, 19 top, 20 left), on the other hand, have a thick shell and a small narrow foot. The conch can use its sickle-shaped operculum, which is attached at the base of the muscular foot, as a "walking stick" to hop along the sandy shore.

The Egg Shell, or Egg Cowrie (pl. 35) has a smooth, porcellaneous shell. The shell is pure white with a high gloss. In life the black mantle of the animal envelops its shell when the mollusk is active. Related to the Egg Cowrie are the true cowries (see pls. 111, 174, and 175). Shown in color in plate 111 (top) is Howell's Cowrie, a rather rare form from Southeastern Australia. Novices sometimes mistake the very common Egg Shell, which occurs throughout the tropical Indo-Pacific region for this species.

Among the 200-odd species of cowries, the Golden Cowrie (pl. 111 bottom) of the South Pacific has long been highly prized because of its rarity and beauty. Specimens were pierced and worn as pendants by the Fijan chiefs. With the arrival of the Europeans, the natives learned that these shells were more valuable for trade if not punched and have largely abandoned the custom of stringing them. Even in its native habitat this species is seldom taken on the beaches. Specimens are generally found only after storm waves have carried them ashore from the deeper waters off coral reefs, or are collected by divers. The species ranges from the Philippines to Melanesia but is most commonly known from the Fiji, Palau, and Solomon Islands.

Even with the intensive shell collecting undertaken in the Pacific in recent years, the Golden Cowrie remains in great demand. There are probably no more than one hundred specimens in American museums, but there are also at least this number in private American collections. During the "golden age" of conchology, 1850–1880, specimens sold in Europe for more than an hundred dollars, a sum equivalent to about three hundred dollars today. Fine specimens, when available, sell for three to four hundred dollars on the American market. At a recent shell auction in London, one brought more than four hundred dollars after spirited bidding.

Other rarities, such as the Guttate Cowrie, Broderip's Cowrie, Brindled Cowrie, Fulton's Cowrie, and Langfords Cowrie, are less commonly seen in collections and also are avidly pursued by collectors.

Probably the most coveted shell was the once-rare Glory-of-the-Sea Cone, which until recently would bring at auction more than a thousand dollars for a good specimen. This cone possesses a legendary quality dating from the middle sixteenth century when the first specimens were brought to Europe from the South Seas. For more than two centuries this slender, tent-patterned cone was considered the most desirable shell in European cabinets, and the few specimens then in collections commanded great admiration and were sold to a succession of wealthy collectors. Fewer than twenty specimens were recorded at the end of the last century, and several of these were lost during the world wars of the twentieth century.

In the postwar period additional specimens were

collected in the Philippine and Coral Seas. As recently as 1967, however, there were believed to be only sixty-three specimens in private and institutional collections of the world.

In the past few years, divers have taken this cone in greatly increasing numbers from waters off the coral reefs fringing the islands of Melanesia. One diver alone reported to have found in the Solomon Islands in a period of less than two years more than eighty specimens, ranging in size from tiny juveniles to large, fully grown ones. Now considerably more than two hundred specimens are known, but the Glory-of-the-Sea Cone still commands the interest of collectors because of its past lore. Specimens have been obtained in recent years in the Philippines, Yap, Indonesia, New Guinea, and especially in the Bismarck Archipelago and the Solomon Islands.

A closely related species, the Bengalese Cone, was recently discovered and described from the Bay of Bengal. Known from only a few specimens, this form and the rare Milne-Edward's Cone, also from the Indian Ocean, now command the highest prices for the cones. Other rare cones include the Stag Cone, Thoma's Cone, Crocate Cone, Matchless Cone (pl. 165 bottom left), Rhododendron Cone, Zonate Cone, and Aurisiacus Cone, most of which live in the Indo-Pacific faunal Province.

The Heliotrope Star Shell (pl. 17), a circular shell with evenly spaced projections, occurs in deep, cold water. The first specimens were taken to England at the time of Captain Cook's voyages and proved to be one of the most popular of shells.

Mangrove swamps and estuarine mud flats are the homes of mollusks which have adapted to a rather rigorous environment where silt and fresh water intermix with salt water. Mollusks living in this type of habitat must have a tolerance for low salinity. During low water they are exposed to the heat of the sun. The Queensland Creeper (pl. 36 left) is an example of a mud-flat denizen. On the other side of the world, in West Africa, the curiously shaped Dusky Creeper (pl. 36 right) occurs in estuaries of rivers flowing into the Atlantic.

Offshore the Neptune's Volute (pl. 25 top), one of a group of snails characteristic of West African waters, glides along on its large, muscular foot in search of prey. Occupying similar habitats in coastal waters off Brazil and Uruguay, Dufresne's Volute (pl. 28 left) is noted for the variation within a species. Its shell may be short and blunt or long and tapering. A projecting callus may be developed on the spire. Coloration may vary from light flesh color to dark brown. The body callus may be deposited over marine growths on the shell.

Sea snails with long, tapered shells that resemble one another superficially but are not closely related are the augers (pl. 24) and the screw shells (pl. 28 right). The latter, which, incidentally, derived their vernacular name from a resemblance to Archimedes' screw, are herbivores and inhabitants of shallow water. The wentletraps (pl. 37 left) have shells with regularly spaced, raised axial ribs. A few species, like the one shown here, possess cancellated sculpture. They live from shallow water down to considerable depths, and some species are believed to be parasitic on sea anemones. The augers (pls. 12 far left to right center and 24) and the turrid shells (pls. 12 far right and 13), together with the cone shells, are families that possess highly developed poison glands. The slender auger shells may be highly pigmented, and most species inhabit shallow warm water. The turrids belong to the largest family of marine snails, with representatives in all seas. They are found from the intertidal zone down to abyssal depths. Few species are colorful. The majority of turrids are small to minute in size.

24.   Triseriate Auger (16–39)
25 top.   Neptune's Volute (15–28)
25 bottom.   Spindle Egg Shell (10–6)
26 top and middle left.   Mawe's Latiaxis (13–43)
26 top right.   Kawamura's Latiaxis (13–46)
26 bottom left and right.   Lischke's Latiaxis (13–48)
27 top.   Kira's Latiaxis (13–47)
27 bottom left.   Santa Rosa Murex (13–31)
27 bottom right.   Pilsbry's Latiaxis (13–44)
28 left.   Dufresne's Volute (15–26)
28 right.   Great Screw Shell (6–1)
29.   Arthritic Spider (9–18)
30 top right.   Deer Antler Murex (13–11)
30 left center.   Ternispine Murex (13–5)
30 long diagonal.   Spindle Tibia (9–9)
30 bottom.   Martini's Tibia (9–10)
31 top.   Lavender Spindle (10–7)
31 center.   Wavy Clio (18–1)
31 bottom.   Three-toothed Cavoline (18–2)

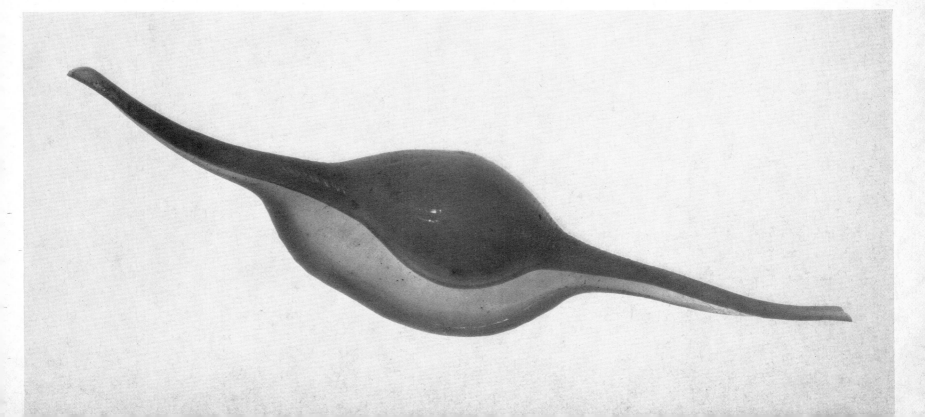

26
◄ *Latiaxis mawae* Griffith and Pidgeon (13–43)

Latiaxis lischkeanus Dunker (13–48) ▲

26
Latiaxis kawamurai Kuroda (13–46) ▲

26
Latiaxis lischkeanus Dunker (13–48) ▼

◄ *Latiaxis lischkeanus* Dunker (13–48)

26

27
Latiaxis kirana
Kuroda
(13–47) ▶

27
Maxwellia santarosana Dall (13–31) ▼

27
Latiaxis pilsbryi Hirase (13–44) ▼

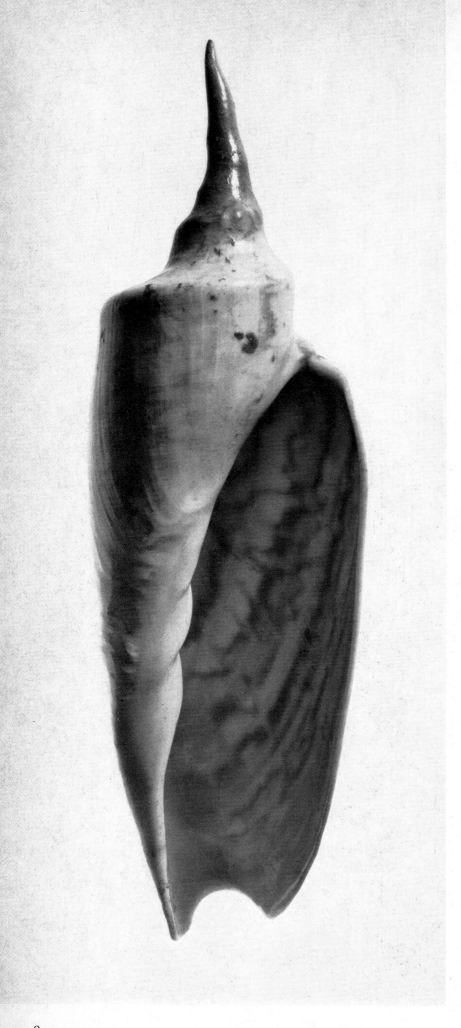

28
Zidona dufresnei Donovan (15–26) ▲

28
Turritella terebra Linné (6–1) ▲

29
Lambis chiragra arthritica Röding (9–18) ▶

30 left center
Murex ternispina Lamarck (13–5)

30 top right
Murex cervicornis Lamarck (13–11)

30 bottom
Tibia martinii Marrat (9–10)

30 long diagonal
Tibia fusus Linné (9–9)

31 top
Volva birostris Linné (10–7)

31 center
Clio recurvum Children (18–1)

31 bottom
Cavolina tridentata Forskål (18–2)

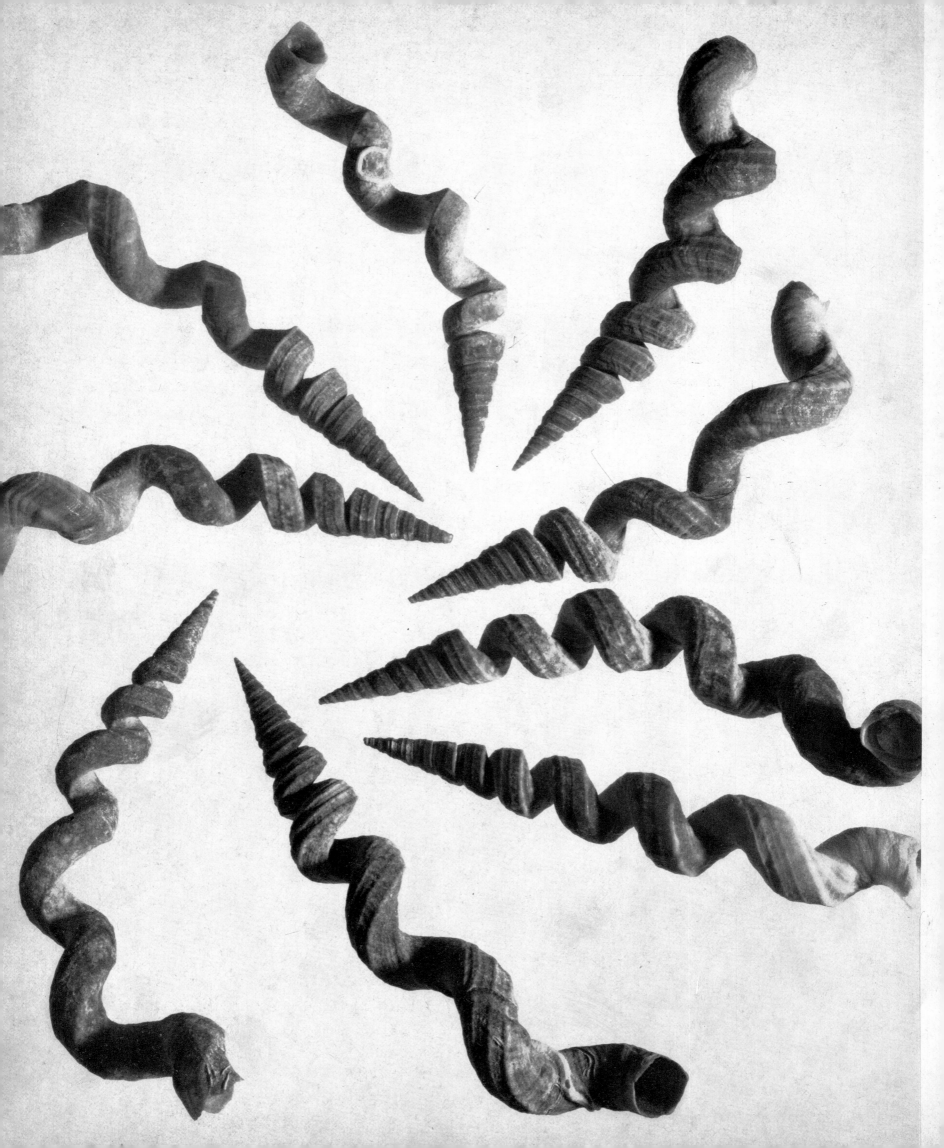

Very curious are the worm shells (pl. 32), which begin life with a regular, spiral shell like that of a screw shell. They live attached to rocks, and are intertwined into compact clusters. As they grow, their shells become twisted and distorted. The lovely latiaxis snails, or coral shells, as they and related groups are known, inhabit coral reefs. Most species live in the Indo-Pacific, while a few occur in the east Pacific, west Atlantic, and Mediterranean. Few reach a height of two inches, but nearly all of them have exquisite white shells with delicate petal-like projections (pls. 26 and 27 top and bottom right). Since they lack a radula, they are believed to be parasitic on coral polyps. Dolphin snails (pl. 8) are also inhabitants of coral reefs, whereas the Lavender Spindle (pl. 31 top) adheres to the stalks of similarly colored soft corals, such as sea fans, the polyps of which it eats.

Murex shells also occur in infinite variety and shapes. They are voracious feeders on bivalves and whatever prey they can overpower. Most species are bottom dwellers. Some abrade their shells as they drag them along on gravel bottoms, much to the disappointment of shell collectors. The delicate Deer Antler Murex (pls. 30 top right and 147) of Northern Australia inhabits crevices in coral, and the Great Stag Antler Murex (pl. 155) of the same area may be found adhering to the undersides of fan coral.

Vastly different in habitat from any of the preceding are the pteropods or sea butterflies (p. 31 center and bottom). Rather than creeping over the substrate as do most marine snails, they have wing-like flaps that permit them to dart rapidly through the water. They are denizens of the open seas, though their glassy shells are occasionally washed ashore on beaches.

The giant squids (genus *Architeuthis*) also are pelagic, inhabiting the depths of the open seas. They are the largest of the living mollusks. Many reports of "sea serpents" probably were the result of observations of these squids during their infrequent appearances at the surface of the sea.

Only occasionally are giant squids cast ashore. However, in the 1870s numerous specimens were stranded along the coast of Newfoundland. Such a phenomenon did not reoccur there until the 1960s. Much of the available information on giant squids has been derived from these Newfoundland specimens.

Harpooned sperm whales commonly regurgitate fragmental specimens, and rarely an entire specimen is found in the gastrointestinal tract of this whale. The largest documented specimen is one found in New Zealand that measures 57 feet in overall length. Another specimen, encountered off the Canary Islands, was estimated to have weighed two tons. Little is known of the natural history of giant squids. They are assumed to be carnivores that feed upon fish and crustaceans. There are reliable accounts of attacks upon ships and seamen.

The giant squids (several species are recognized) were known to the early ubiquitous Scandinavians as "kraken." They were evidently encountered and feared by the Mediterranean sailors several centuries B.C. It was not until the latter part of the nineteenth century, however, that the nature of this "mystery of the deep" became generally known to the scientific world.

Cone Shells: The Snail with the Deadly Bite

The 400-odd species of cone shells are equipped with a potent venom and a dartlike radular delivery apparatus that enable them to paralyze and consume fish, worms, or other mollusks, depending on the food preference of each species. Human fatalities have resulted from their deadly bite. The cones have been called the scorpions or rattlesnakes of the molluscan world.

The first recorded death of a person who carelessly handled one of these poisonous snails occurred in 1705, when the Dutch naturalist G. E. Rumphius reported that a woman on Banda Island, Indonesia, had died after holding a living cone in her hand. She had picked up the pretty shell while fishing and felt a faint stinging in her hand. Within a short time she became unconscious and was dead. Other human deaths have subsequently been reported. Although the bite of these snails is not always fatal to humans, they should be handled cautiously for they are potentially dangerous to man.

The weapon that inflicts injury is a modified radular tooth in the form of a hollow chitinous needle which is elaborately barbed and knobbed. These tiny radular teeth, less than a tenth of an inch long, have evolved as harpoons laden with venom for the killing of the cone's prey. Each species of cone manufactures a venom peculiar to that species and adapted for a particular food preference, be it fish, worm, or other mollusk. In most instances the venom is specific for the snail's habitual prey. The Geographic Cone, for example, kills fish but not other kinds of prey. The Textile Cone (pl. 101 middle left) and the Marbled Cone (pl. 100 right) kill only gastropods, and the Lividus Cone only worms. In some species the venoms appear to be host specific and only are effective against certain species of fish, worms, or other mollusks.

Most cones are nocturnal in habit and hunt at night. Lying buried in sand until a prey animal approaches, they apparently can sense its presence by means of a chemical sensor which is ejected into the water through the snail's siphon. When the prey approaches, the cone dispatches it with one or more darts. If the victim is a worm, only one dart is usually needed, but those cones that consume other snails may eject as many as six darts into the prey. The victim of the worm-eating cones is paralyzed and engulfed by the snail's mouth and is passed into the oral cavity. The radular dart remains in the worm and moves through the digestive tract. The snail-eating cones first paralyze the prey and then place their mouth against the prey's aperture. After a period of time, which may last up to one hour, the predator consumes the soft parts of the victim and moves away from the empty shell of the snail. The most elaborate hunting behavior is exhibited by the fish-eating cones, such as the Striate Cone (pl. 165 bottom right). This cone lives on sandy bottoms with only its siphon protruding. As a fish approaches, the cone extends its proboscis in the direction of the prey. When the fish comes within range of the proboscis, the snail ejects a single dart into it and then swallows the paralyzed fish by expanding its mouth to engulf the victim in the oral cavity.

It is the venom of the fish-eating cones that is injurious to other vertebrates, including man. The Geographic Cone is generally considered to be the most dangerous to humans, but the venom of other species may be equally deadly. Although the only recorded human fatalities have occurred in the South Pacific, collectors in other areas should use care in handling cones, especially those with large shells.

Giant Clams and Other Bivalves

Although not as numerous as the sea snails, the marine bivalves make up an exceedingly diverse class. Many species of clams are able to dig or creep along by using their muscular foot. Scallops and a few others are able to propel themselves through the water. By snapping their valves, they expel water and progress by a sort of erratic jet propulsion. Many kinds of bivalves are cemented into place. Among those that are permanently fixed are to be found some of the most bizarre and remarkable species. Projecting spines, lamellations, and flutings are some of the adornments that have been developed.

Thorny oysters (pl. 42) settle on dead coral, submerged wood or other hard surfaces when small. As they mature, long flattened spines are produced. One of the most remarkable bivalves is the Lazarus' Jewel Box (pl. 47), whose tightly packed spines resemble some sort of leafy vegetable.

Another sessile bivalve, the Giant Clam, *Tridacna gigas* Linné, is the largest living species of bivalve mollusk, attaining a length of more than four feet. The valves of a specimen on display in the American Museum of Natural History, excluding the soft parts, weigh nearly 589 pounds. This specimen was collected in the Philippine Islands in 1906. This species of giant clam is restricted to the tropical waters of the Pacific Ocean, from the Philippine Islands to Micronesia, living in association with reef corals. These bivalves, of which five living species are recognized, occur only in the tropical Indo-Pacific faunal Province.

In life the juveniles are attached to coral by gelat-

32.   West Indian Worm Shell (6–3)
33.   Watering Pot (35–1)
34.   Rose-branch Murex (13–15)
35.   Egg Cowrie (10–5)
36 left.   Queensland Creeper (6–4)
36 right.   Dusky Creeper (6–5)
37 left.   Magnificent Wentletrap (7–2)
37 right.   Giant Creeper (6–8)
38.   Root Murex (13–26)
39.   Black-lined Limpet (2–1)

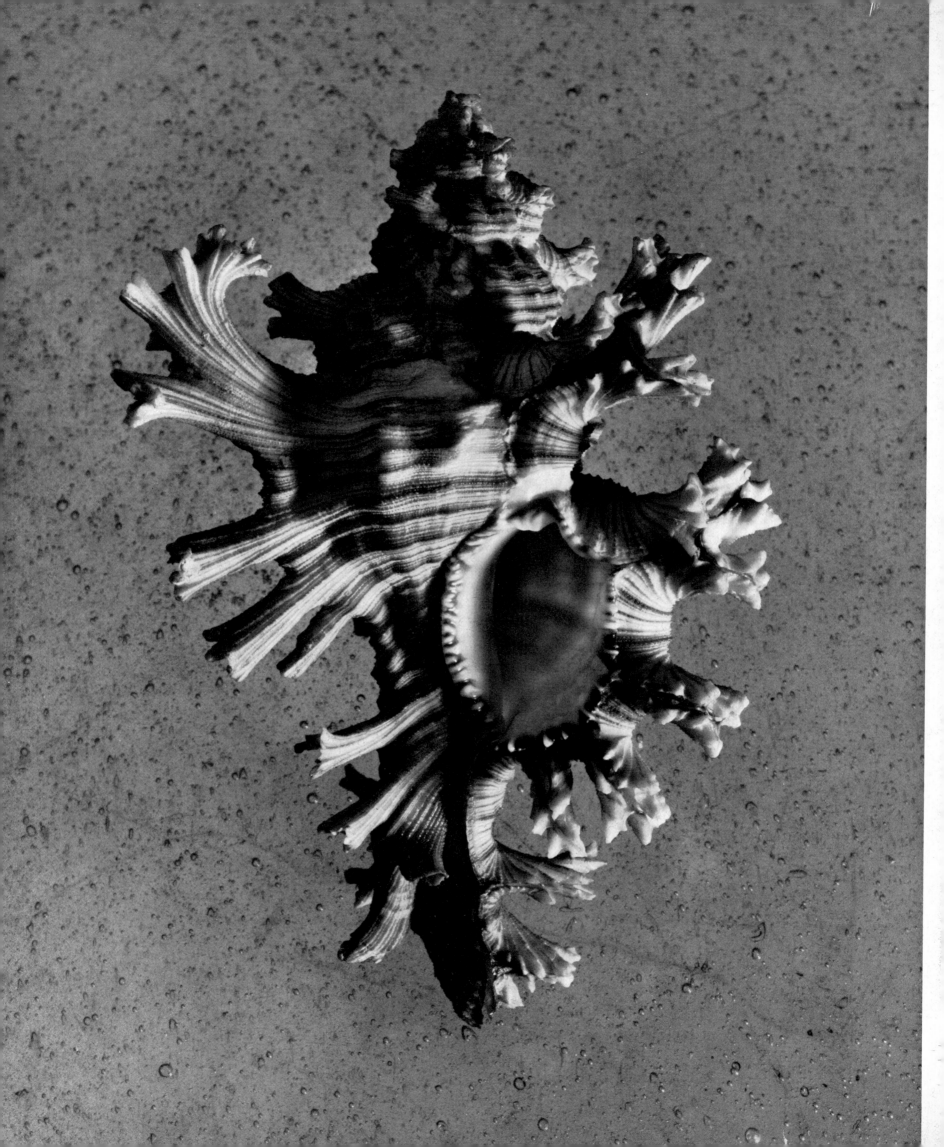

34
◀ *Chicoreus palmarosae* Lamarck (13–15)

35
Ovula ovum Linné (10–5) ▲

36 left
Pyrazus eberninus Bruguière (6–4)

36 right
Tympanotomus fuscatus Linné (6–5)

37 left
Amaea magnifica Sowerby (7–2)

37 right
Campanile symbolicum Tate (6–8)

38
Muricanthus radix Gmelin (13–26) ▲

39
Cellana nigrolineata Reeve (2–1) ▶

inous byssal anchors. At maturity the anchor is lost and the shell depends on weight alone to anchor itself in position on the reef. The fleshy mantle is expanded when the valves are open to expose the thickened mantle edge, in which unicellular, symbiotic algae, called zooxanthellae, are "farmed" as a supplementary source of food.

Contrary to popular belief, the giant clams are not known to have caused the death by drowning of divers who accidentally placed an arm or leg between the valves. The valves close very slowly when the clam is disturbed, as the mantle, which is filled with water, must be withdrawn. The giant clams, therefore, do not merit the title of "man eater." A small specimen of the Fluted Giant Clam is shown in plate 46.

Along the Atlantic seaboard of the United States, the delicate and beautiful Angel's Wing (pl. 40) may be found. When small, Angel's Wings excavate a burrow in mud or other substrates, in which they pass their lives. They feed by projecting their siphon up their tunnel and drawing in sea water, from which they filter organic particles.

The Gaper Clams are members of the surf clam family and live in depths of three feet or more in fine sand or firm, sandy mud in bays, sloughs, and estuaries as well as in quieter, sheltered areas in depths of a hundred feet or more along the outer coast from Alaska to Monterey, California. The siphon forms a long tube which extends to the surface of the substrate. When the substrate is exposed at low tide, the siphon makes a round depression at the surface. If the clam is disturbed, the siphon is withdrawn rapidly enough to squirt water several feet into the air. The shell attains a length of ten inches. This clam is highly esteemed for food. It is used commercially in the making of chowder and is the object of an active sports fishery in California. Unfortunately, clam diggers are threatening to exterminate the intertidal populations.

Perhaps the most curious of all bivalves is the peculiar group known under the vernacular name of Watering Pot Shells. They begin life as typical clams and excavate a burrow as does the Angel's Wing. As the tiny clams mature, they begin to form a cylindrical calcareous tube. When the tube is completed, the upper or open end may have a series of rufflelike flutes (pl. 33). The minute valves of the juvenile clam are preserved on the surface of the tube. The lower end has a ruffle around the margin and perforations in the central portion which impart the appearance of the spout of an old-fashioned watering can. The surface of the tube may be covered with pebbles and sand grains.

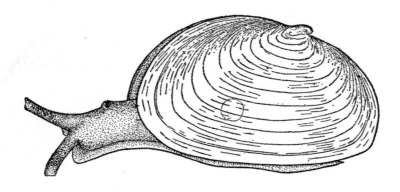

The strange bivalved gastropod *Berthelinia* resembles a clam with the head of a snail and was classified with the bivalves before living animals revealed their true identity. (After S. Kawaguti and T. Yamasu, 1959.)

The discovery in 1959 of an extraordinary little green snail with two shells, a bivalved gastropod, has been the subject of considerable attention. The top of one valve has the normal spiral coiling of a snail, while the other valve develops from a lobe on the left side of the aperture (see the accompanying figure). This snail, known as *Berthelinia*, lives on seaweeds in warmer waters from Africa, India, Australia, and Japan to California, Panama, and the West Indies. In California occurs a small clam which has internal valves that are covered by the animal's soft parts. This mollusk, called *Chlamydoconcha*, meaning appropriately "cloaked shell," swims by vigorously moving its muscular foot, and it could be mistaken for a snail. Thus, it might be called a "gastropod-bivalve."

The heart cockle shells (pls. 41 and 45 bottom) are related to the large Cardiums, which have oval, heart-shaped shells. In the present group, the two valves are laterally compressed, with a strong keel around the margin. Since the two valves separate in the middle, one species is sometimes called, perhaps facetiously, the Broken Heart Cockle.

The familiar Jingle Shells of the American Atlantic seaboard have a large opening in the lower valve, through which the solid, pluglike byssus protrudes, attaching them firmly to a rock or another shell. Related to the Jingle Shells are the Saddle Oyster and Window Pane Shells of the Western Pacific. Lacking a byssus, they live in colonies on muddy bottoms of bays. Both groups have thin, brittle shells of a micalike consistency. Neither is good to eat.

The Saddle Oyster (pl. 44 bottom) has little economic use other than its value to shell collectors and in novelty manufacture. The Window Pane Shells are utilized in the manufacture of artistic shellcraft products such as screens, lamp shades, jewelry boxes, and table tops. As the name implies, these shells are also used in a most unique way, as window panes: in the Philippines quantities of the translucent shells are arranged in rows with leadings of wood or bamboo strips to make windows.

41
Glossus vulgaris Reeve (29–3)

42
Spondylus americanus Hermann (25–11)

43
Callanaitis disjecta Perry (30–7) ▲

44
Anadara granosa Linné
(22–2)

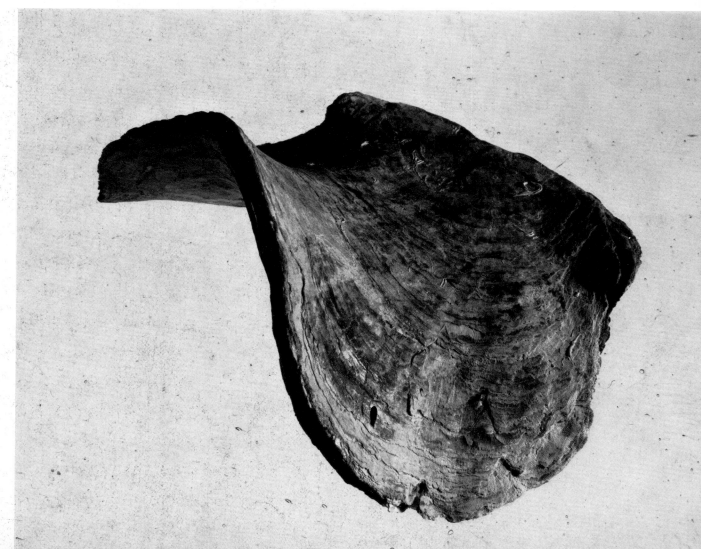

44
Placuna sella Linné
(26–1)

45
Pecten jacobeus Linné
(25–8 a)

45
Corculum cardissa Linné
(29–4)

46
Tridacna maximus Röding (29–5) ▲

47
Chama lazarus Linné (28–1) ▶

III.
Carrier Shells

The carrier shells are known as "the original shell collectors," for these gastropods commonly cement dead shells and other extraneous objects such as small pebbles, bits of coral, and minerals to the top and sides of their own shells. This curious habit was evolved more than 100 million years ago. The foreign objects serve to reinforce the carrier shell and apparently provide a protective camouflage to hide the mollusk from predators. When viewed from the top or side, the living carrier shell may resemble a pile of dead shells or a heap of rocky rubble. These snails have been given the appropriate generic name *Xenophora*, from the Greek forms *xeno-*, meaning "stranger" or "foreigner," and *-phora*, meaning "carrier." The only other gastropods known to have developed the collecting habit were Paleozoic euomphalid snails, which became extinct some 220 million years ago.

As the carrier snail grows by adding newly secreted material to the outer edge of the body whorl of its shell, it picks up the dead shells or other foreign objects and holds them by the edge of its mantle to the new part of its shell. In a short time the objects become firmly cemented to the periphery of the growing whorl of the shell, where they remain permanently attached, becoming part of the surface ornamentation. The foreign particles are placed on the shell in positions that do not impede the movement of the living mollusk. The selection of objects appears to be made at random, depending on what debris is nearby on the sea floor. Not all species of *Xenophora* collect extraneous objects. The shells of these species, devoid of decorations, resemble thin top shells of the family Trochidae; but the interior of the carrier shells is porcellaneous rather than pearly like the top shells, and the operculum is fan-shaped rather than circular in outline.

These "collections" provide an interesting variety of combinations and arrangements of the dead shells of other snails, clams, oysters, scallops, corals, and different kinds of rocks and minerals. On occasion, very rare shells, some new to science, have been found attached to these gastropods, especially those living in extreme depths of the oceans. Most of the approximately forty species are found in tropical waters, although some live in the Mediterranean Sea and off New Zealand, South Australia, and South Africa.

◀ *Xenophora pallidula* Reeve (9–3)

The specimens of carrier shells shown here exhibit a representative sample of the artistry of these mollusks. The Pallid Carrier (pls. 48, 51 top and bottom, 54 top, 55) has collected pebbles, corals, and various kinds of snails and clams, including, in one specimen (pls. 54 top, 55), a single species of Bittersweet Clam. The Wrinkled Carrier (pls. 49, 52, 53 bottom) has attached different types of pebbles, together with shells of cones and oysters; one specimen (pls. 52, 53 bottom) also has served for the attachment of living corals and wormtube-like gastropods. Longley's Carrier (pl. 50) has utilized turrid and volute snails; while the Mexican Carrier (pl. 53 top) has cemented clams and oysters, upon which are seen colonies of mosslike animals, bryozoans. The Peron's Carrier (pl. 54 bottom) has collected only pebbles.

48. Pallid Carrier (9–3)
49. Wrinkled Carrier (9–6)
50. Longley's Carrier (9–2)
51 top, bottom.   Pallid Carrier (9–3)
52, 53 bottom.   Wrinkled Carrier (9–6)
53 top.   Mexican Carrier (9–4)
54 top, 55.   Pallid Carrier (9–3)
54 bottom.   Peron's Carrier (9–5)

49
Xenophora corrugata Reeve (9–6) ▶

50 (all 3)
Tugurium longleyi
Bartsch (9–2)

51 (both)
Xenophora pallidula
Reeve (9–3)

53
▲ *Xenophora robusta* Verrill (9–4)

52
◄ *Xenophora corrugata* Reeve (9–6)

53
Xenophora corrugata Reeve (9–6) ►

54
▲ *Xenophora pallidula* Reeve
(9–3)

55
Xenophora pallidula Reeve
(9–3) ▶

54
◀ *Xenophora peronianus* Iredale
(9–5)

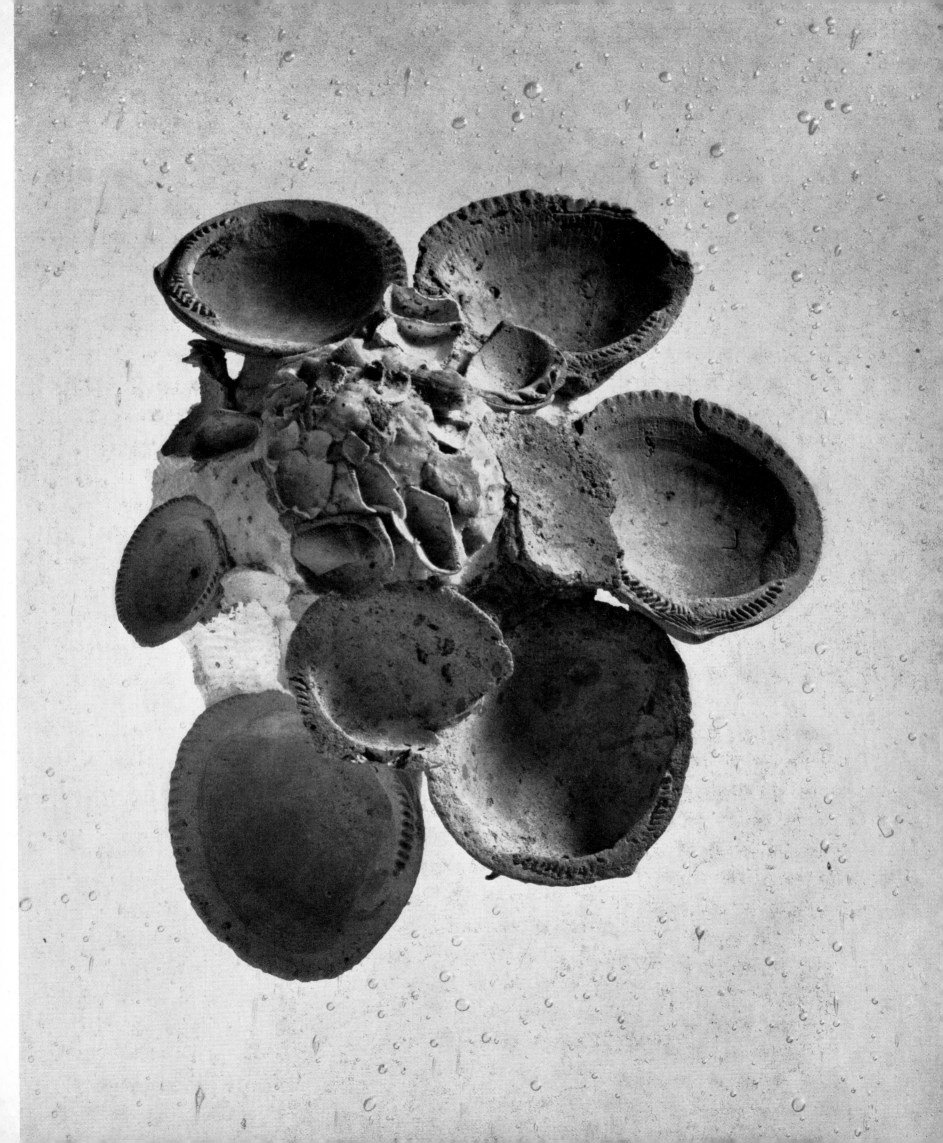

IV.
Structure of Shells

As we have seen, the shells of mollusks occur in a vast array of sizes and shapes, but the apparent diversity of structural form displayed by their shells reflects a common architectural plan. The gastropod shell is typically an elongated cone wound into a spiral around a central axis, the columella. The surface of this pillar, to which the columellar muscles of the mollusk body are attached, may be smooth, as in Troschel's Murex (pl. 58 top left), or may possess screwlike ribbing to provide additional surface in some instances for the attachment of the columellar muscles, as in the case of West Indian Chanks (pl. 56). The turns of the spiral, the whorls, are demarcated by lines known as sutures. The sutural lines may be smooth, wavy, irregular, or somewhat indented. In most species the whorls are in close contact, with each whorl being partly covered by the succeeding larger whorl. In some species some or all of the whorls are disconnected, as in the loosely coiled vermetid snails (pl. 32), which, when fully grown, resemble uncoiled worm tubes. The largest whorl, termed the body whorl, bounds the aperture, the large opening through which the foot and anterior part of the body of the snail can be protruded and retracted. The edge of the aperture, which may possess small denticles, is termed the outer lip, and the opposite wall, which is continuous with the columella, is called the inner lip. The base of the body whorl and aperture may be extended into a tube of varied length, termed the siphonal canal, to accommodate the siphon, if one is present. A small posterior canal may occur at the upper end of the aperture. The smaller whorls above the body whorl form the spire of the shell, terminating at the apex. The apex represents the larval shell, which may differ in sculpture from the succeeding whorls. A hole, the umbilicus, is produced adjacent to the aperture in the axis of the shell when the larger whorls fail to maintain contact centrally. Nearly every conceivable variant of this nor-

mal conical shape occurs in the gastropod shell, as exemplified by the photographs in this chapter and those of preceding chapters. In some groups, such as the nudibranchs, a shell is lacking; it may be reduced or completely lost in cases of extreme parasitism. In life, the snail moves with the shell carried with the aperture forward; thus the aperture is considered the anterior end of the shell.

In the bivalves, the shell consists of two usually convex valves of various shapes. The paired valves open and close by hinging on one side. The structures involved in this function are collectively known as the hinge. In most bivalves the hinge occupies a dorsal position in relation to the soft anatomy, and the opposite margin, which opens the valves most widely, is ventral. The end of the shell closest to the mouth is anterior; the opposite end, being nearest to the anus, is posterior. Generally speaking, although there are exceptions, the hinge area is regarded as dorsal. The dorsally placed noselike beak, containing the larval shell, or prodissoconch, is usually situated nearer the anterior end of the shell than the posterior end. "Umbo" is frequently used as a synonym of "beak," though specialists make a technical distinction in the application of the two terms.

Starting with the prodissoconch, growth of a bivalve shell proceeds by successive additions to the shell along the margins of the two valves. The additions are broadest in a direction determined by the shape of the adult shell and narrowest close to the dorsal margin, where they converge from either end toward the beak. Indications of the successive increments to the valves are commonly preserved on the surface of the valves. In cases where the beak occurs close to the midpoint of the dorsal surface in the adult specimen, as in the scallops, the shell is termed equilateral. The shell is described as inequilateral if the beak lies closer to one end or the other, as in the Hard-shell Clam (pl. 59) for example. The term "terminal" is used for shells in which the beak occurs on the most anterior or posterior point of the valve, as in the Winged Tree-Oyster (pl. 61 right).

In life, the valves are closed by one or two adductor muscles and are held open by a chitinous ligament, which varies considerably in size and shape. The ligament is an elastic band and springs the valves open when the animal relaxes or dies. The interlocking teeth in the hinge of each valve serve to strengthen the attachment of the valves and to keep the valves in natural alignment.

The bivalves exhibit a great variety in the structural pattern of the hinge. The arrangement of the hinge teeth has been used to classify bivalves. Some groups, especially primitive ones, are without hinge teeth, but dentition is present in the hinges of most species. Many descriptive terms are applied to the various kinds of hinge structure. One of the more simple types of dentition, termed taxodont (meaning "a line of teeth"), consists of a series of short, straight or chevron-shaped teeth that occupy the entire length of the dorsal margin of the valve. An example of taxodont dentition is seen in the ark clams, as illustrated by *Anadara* (pl. 60). This type of tooth structure has evolved independently in several groups of bivalves, including species inhabiting fresh water. The American Thorny Oyster (pl. 61 left) exhibits another type of dentition, termed isodont (meaning "equal-toothed"). In this type there are two equal teeth in each valve, placed symmetrically on either side of a triangular or rounded pit and received in corresponding sockets in the other valve. The Winged Tree-Oyster (pl. 61 right) presents an interesting example of a species lacking hinge teeth in the adult shell. Instead the hinge is occupied by multiple ligamental grooves. Hinge teeth are present in the earliest growth stages of these tree-oysters, but are replaced by the ligamental grooves as the shell increases in size.

Mollusks have evolved numerous ways to strengthen the shell. The surface may be corrugated (pl. 71), ribbed (pl. 60), or otherwise modified structurally. The valves may be twisted (pl. 66) or convoluted in various forms (pls. 64, 65).

In some gastropods the young stage of the shell lacks apertural dentition. For example, the immature bulla stage of the cowries is fragile and thin-lipped, somewhat resembling an olive shell. As growth proceeds, the shell becomes thickened and the outer lip becomes curled in and takes the form of the mature cowrie shell. At maturity, teeth are formed along both sides of the aperture and the spire becomes embedded in shelly material. The immature stage of the stromb conch and spider shells are spindle-shaped and lack the apertural dentition and broad, heavy lip of the mature forms (pls. 75, 76). In other gastropods, notably the murex, the teeth or thickenings that were deposited on the former apertural sites may be entirely reabsorbed by the mantle as growth of the shell proceeds and subsequent apertural structures are produced (pl. 70).

Certain gastropods absorb the internal portions of the whorls and the associated parts of the columellar axis. As a result of this process the shell is no longer a spiral but becomes more or less a produced cone, and the viscera contained in the spire may lose their spiral form. This condition is known to occur in the adult stages of nerites, olives, and cowries among the marine gastropods. In the cones, the internal walls of the spire are commonly reduced by absorption to thin partitions by the time the mollusk has reached maturity. The absorption of the internal structures results in a reduction of the weight of the shell as it increases in size.

Typically the molluscan shell consists of a thin outer organic layer of "skin," the periostracum, and of three structured calcareous layers comprising an outer prismatic layer, a middle lamellar layer, and an inner porcellaneous layer. The two prominent limy layers of the bivalve shell are exposed to view on a worn valve of the Hard-shell Clam (pl. 59). The number of calcareous layers may vary, with as many as six being present in some gastropod shells.

The horny periostracum, which is commonly a thin uniform brown covering of the shell, is composed of conchiolin, a form of sclerotized protein, the same material of which the horny opercula of snails are formed. The surface of the periostracum in some gastropods and bivalves is ridged or otherwise ornamented with different kinds of structures, including hairs and bristles, which are more likely to be preserved in the juvenile stage. This outer covering is easily eroded from the surface and can be defec-

56.   West Indian Chank (15–10a)
57.   Humboldt's Creeper (6–6)
58 top left.   Troschel's Murex (13–3)
58 top right.   Great Screw Shell (6–1)
58 bottom.   Northern Moon Snail (11–5)
59.   Hard-shell Clam (30–00)
60.   *Anadara* species (22–00)
61 left.   American Thorny Oyster (25–11)
61 right.   Winged Tree-Oyster (23–1)
62.   *Anadara* Species (22–00)
63.   Smooth Heart Cockle (29–2)

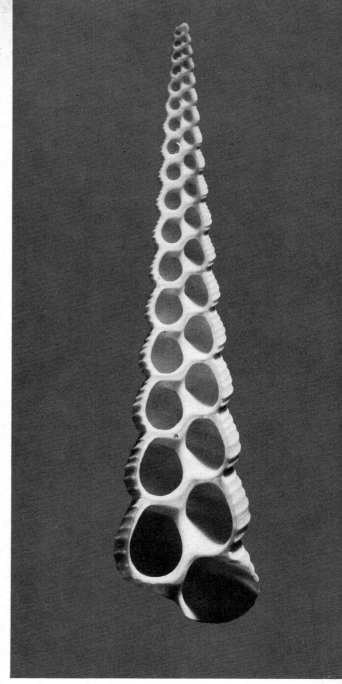

58
Murex troscheli Lischke
(13–3) ▲

58
Turritella terebra Linné
(6–1) ▲

58
Lunatia heros Say
(11–5) ▶

59
Mercenaria mercenaria
Linné (30–00) ▶

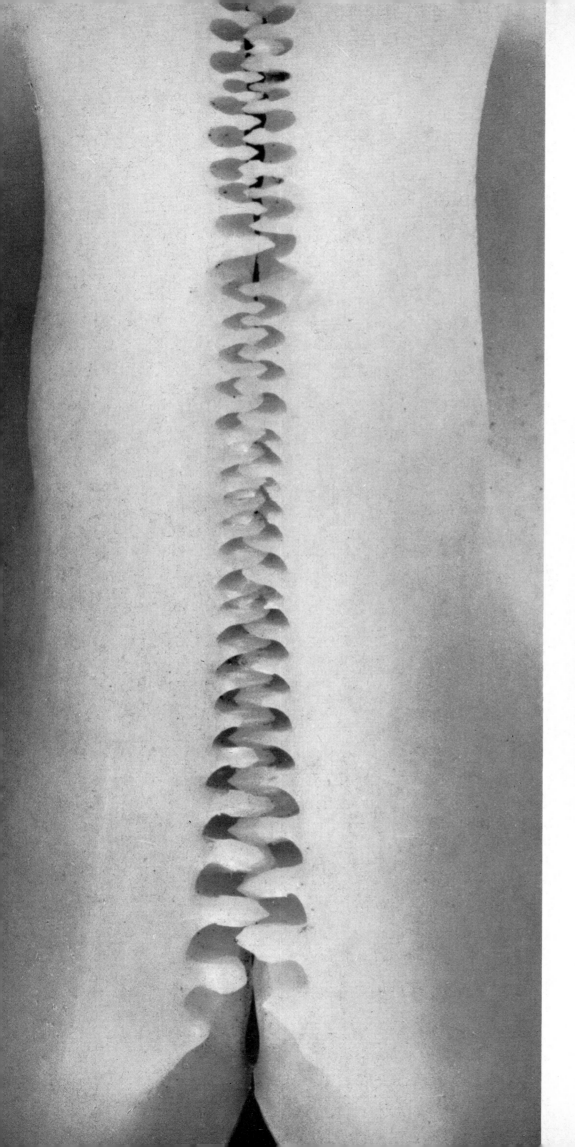

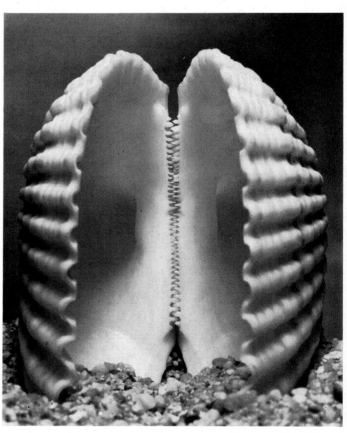

60
◀ *Anadara* sp. (22–00) ▲

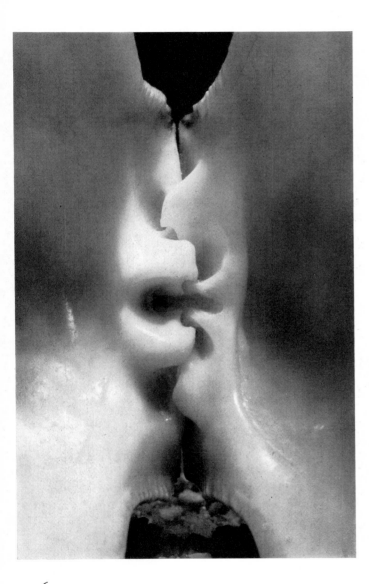

61
▲ *Spondylus americanus* Hermann
(25–11)

61
Isognomon isognomon Linné (23–1) ▶

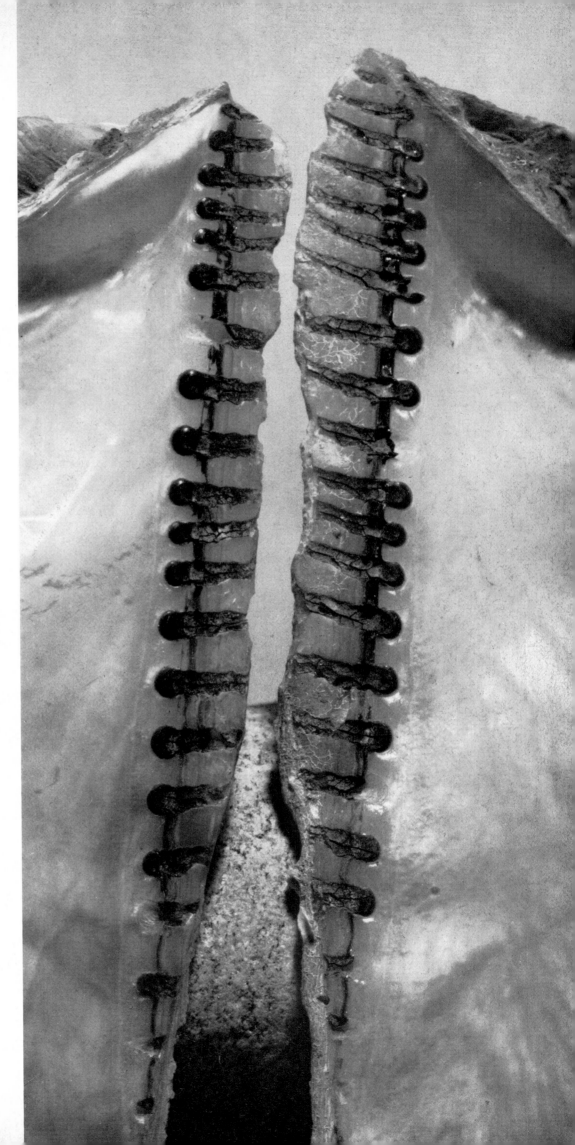

62
◀ *Anadara* sp. (22–00)

63
Glossus humanus Linné (29–2) ▲

tive or poorly preserved on the shells of old specimens. In some groups, for example the cowries, in which the shell is covered by the mantle, the periostracum is wanting. In others, it may be nearly transparent, with the surface color of the shell in evidence. In marine mollusks, it serves to protect the shell from the chemical or solvent action of salt water.

The limy prismatic and lamellar layers in the shells of gastropods and bivalves are composed almost entirely of calcium carbonate in either of two forms, calcite or aragonite, which are chemically identical but belong to different systems of crystallization. Aragonite is less stable than calcite and in fossil shells may transform into calcite. Most gastropods have shells consisting primarily of aragonite, but traces of calcite may be present together with other minerals. In bivalves, both types of calcium carbonate also occur, as well as very small quantities of other minerals. The calcareous layers of the molluscan shell are interleaved with conchiolin. There is some evidence to suggest that the shells of primitive mollusks are largely aragonitic and that calcite appeared in the later stages of molluscan evolution.

Each distinguishable layer of the calcareous wall of the shell is composed of one of the two forms of calcium carbonate in variable structural forms and types. Aragonitic layers generally are lamellate, consisting of rectangular plates arranged like the leaves of a book composed of oblique columns made of calcareous fibers. The obliquity of the columns tends to alternate in the direction of the successive plates, and the resulting structure presented by cross sections of the shell wall differs according to the plane of the section viewed. Calcite is generally prismatic and layers composed of calcite present a more or less prismatic appearance regardless of the plane of section. The crossed layers, especially those of lamellar structure, add strength to the otherwise thin and fragile wall of the shell.

The aragonitic nacreous inner layer consists of thin leaflike crystals aligned nearly parallel to the inner surface of the shell and separated by thin films of conchiolin, which resemble lacework. This lustrous structure, the mother-of-pearl, is best displayed by the shells of the pearl oysters and the abalones (pl. 106). Conchiolin also occurs between the prisms of calcite.

Foliated structure is found in the calcite of some bivalves, in a form similar to that of the aragonitic nacreous layer. It consists of more or less parallel leaves of this mineral, but it differs from the nacreous structure in being coarser and less regular, and it lacks luster.

The operculum, which is secreted and borne by the rear part of the dorsal side of the foot, is usually the only solid accessory to the gastropod shell. The primary function of the operculum is to close the aperture when the body of the mollusk has retreated into the shell. It may fit the apertural opening tightly and serve to protect the soft body. In many forms, for example the cowries, the operculum is greatly reduced in size and does not serve this purpose; it is lacking in the adult stages of some groups, including most of the harps, volutes, tonnids, mitrids, cowries, to mention a few. In other forms, exemplified by the stromb conchs (pl. 104), the narrow, pointed operculum is used as an aid in locomotion – the animal places the tip of the operculum in the substrate and then extends the foot by a sudden movement in such a way that these snails may be said to hop along the bottom. The carrier shells (pls. 48–55) also use the operculum in locomotion.

Most opercula are composed of light horny material of the same type as the "skin" or periostracum coating the shell. But in some snails the operculum is limy, in some cases consisting of massive calcareous bodies, as in the turban shells (pl. 84). Most of the limy opercula conform to the shape of the aperture of the shell. These may be classified into three main structural types: spiral, concentric, or lamellar. Flat and platelike forms are the most common, with conical and cylindrically spiral types rare. The circular, spiral form with numerous volutions is considered to be most primitive. In dextral snails, for example the Variable Turban (pl. 79), if the operculum is spiral, it grows in a direction that is counterclockwise when the outer surface is viewed. In sinistral snails the direction of the opercular growth is opposite. Therefore the presence of a spiral operculum provides a means of distinguishing between the shells of truly sinistral snails and those with falsely sinistral shells, the hyperstrophic shells of snails with dextral anatomy.

The morphological characters of the operculum

may be used to identify the gastropod shell in many instances because of the distinct opercular features found in these species. The outer surface of the operculum of the Turk's Cap (pl. 78), for example, is ornamented with small, pebblelike projections.

Among other accessories to the gastropod shell is the calcareous support secreted by the foot and cemented to the substratum by certain limpetlike marine snails, the hipponicids. These sessile gastropods utilize this structure as an attachment to hold the foot tightly to the rock or other object on which they are adhering. In certain land snails an unusual kind of calcareous structure is developed within the shell. Termed the clausilium, after the generic name of the snail, *Clausilia*, which means "little door" in Latin, it is a narrow, thin, curved plate with a stalklike process at one end which curves around the columella within the aperture. It serves the function of an operculum by sliding into position to close the aperture when the body of the animal is withdrawn into its shell.

An operculum is lacking in most land snails. A temporary covering of the aperture, the epiphragm, is secreted by some of these snails during hibernation or during dry periods when they aestivate. The epiphragm is simply a film of dried slime, which may be supplemented and strengthened by the addition of lime salts. This membrane, which serves as a temporary operculum, is detached and discarded when favorable conditions return and permit the animal to become active again. The epiphragm forms an effective seal to the shell. Some of these snails are reported to have remained in this inactive state for many years.

In those groups of gastropods in which the operculum is smaller than the apertural opening or is not present, the aperture may be partially protected by structural modifications of the shell, such as toothlike projections on the outer and inner lips surrounding the aperture. Among the species illustrated, examples are the Grinning Tun (pl. 77) and the Writhed Distorted Shell (pl. 72).

65
Lopha cristagalli Linné (27–1) ▶

66
◄ *Trisidos tortuosa* Linné (22–1)

67
Scaphander lignarius Linné (17–3) ▲

68
Aulica imperialis Lamarck (15–20)

69
Cassis cornuta Linné (12–1)

70
Murex ramosus Linné (13–14a)

71
Tonna melanostoma Jay (12–10a)

74
▲ *Tibia fusus* Linné (9–9)

75
Lambis chiragra arthritica Röding (9–18) ▶

◀ *Lambis digitata* Perry (9–23)

Malea ringens Swainson (12–10) ▲

78
▲ *Turbo sarmaticus* Linné (3–22)

79
Turbo fluctuosus Wood (3–21) ▶

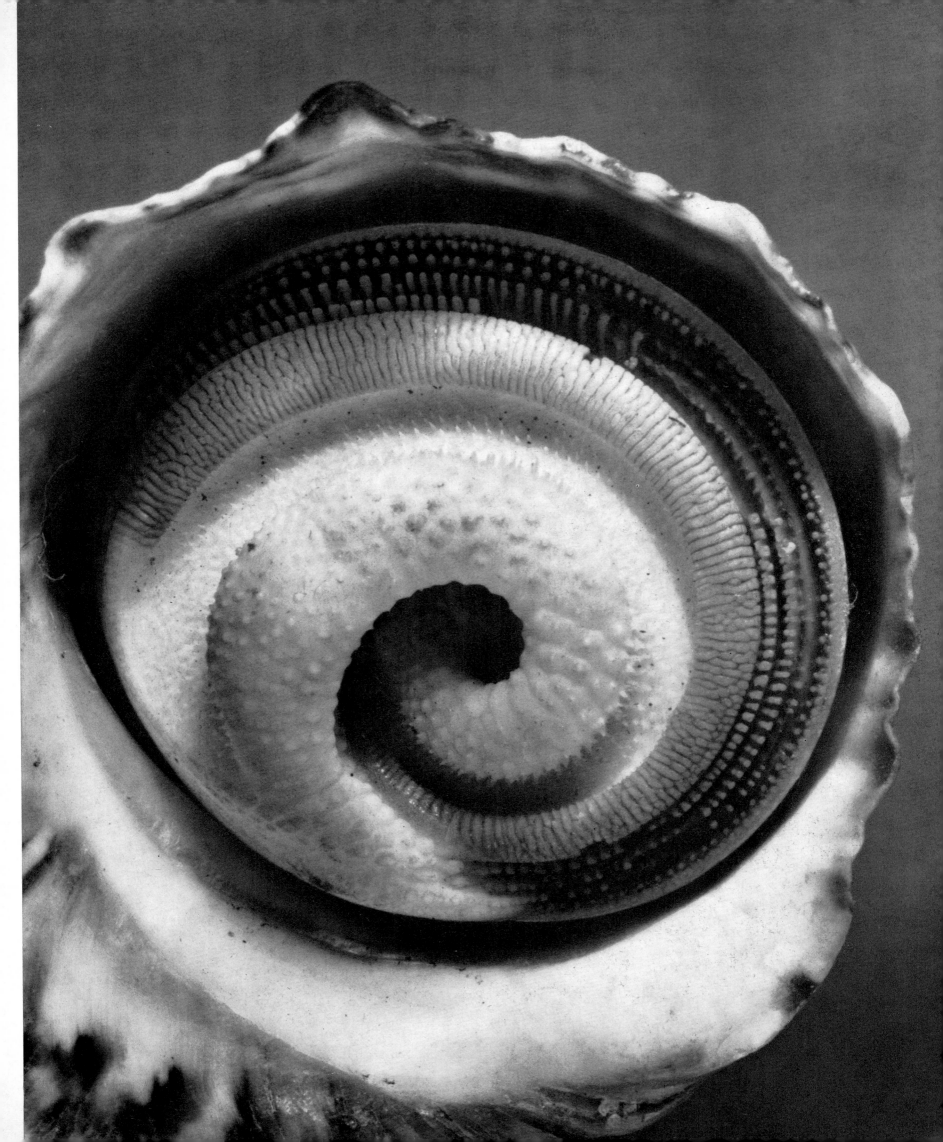

V.
The Spiral

Examples of spiral form in nature are plentifully represented by the varied architecture of the molluscan shell. The shells of marine snails are commonly produced in the form of modified cones, which are spirally coiled, and the resulting shell has become adapted to economize weight and space. This evolutionary process, together with other modifications, has produced a multitude of beautifully formed gastropod shells exhibiting the organic spiral.

The spiral curve may be defined in general terms as a line which, starting from the point of origin, continually diminishes in curvature as it recedes from the original point of growth. The spiral resulting from this growth pattern forms a line in which the radius of curvature continually increases, a logarithmic spiral (pl. 83). This definition excludes the form of the helical "spiral," such as the thread of a screw, which is technically a cylindrical curve. Mathematically speaking, the simple helix or screw is not a spiral but is a curve that neither starts from a definite origin nor varies in its curvature as it proceeds. Such growth curves are also commonly represented in nature – for example, by the "spiral" twist and twine of a climbing stem of a plant.

In the case of the "typical" gastropod shell, the spiral conformation begins with the larval shell, the protoconch. At the termination of the free-swimming veliger stage, the paddlelike lobes of the velum are discarded, and the tiny mollusk starts life crawling on the sea bottom. The minute mollusk rapidly begins to resemble its parents by producing continual additions to the open end, the aperture, until the shell attains full size (pl. 58).

The shells of most marine gastropods coil to the right – that is, the aperture is situated on the right side of the shell when the apex is held upward with the aperture toward the viewer. Such shells are termed dextral. The shells of only a few species of marine snails are naturally left-handed forms, or sinistral (pl. 87 bottom right).

The shells of some gastropods appear to have no whorls. The shell of limpets is a cuplike dome, but in most limpetlike snails, the embryonic shell is spirally coiled. In other flattened gastropod shells, such as the abalone, only the early whorls are raised spirals and these may be worn off the surface of the shell. The various growth stages, however, are rep-

◀ *Conus betulinus* Linné (16–28)

resented on the surface of the abalone shells by lines producing generating curves, the "gnomes" of the pre-existing shell. In many gastropod specimens, the fragile protoconch may be lost through wear of the shell or by reabsorption by the mollusk.

The logarithmic spiral may be beautifully manifested in the "door" or operculum of the gastropods. In the turban shells (pl. 84 bottom), for instance, the operculum is a thick, calcareous structure with a curved outline. The successive increments added to the growing edge of the operculum show a spiral line of growth.

The bivalve mollusks, such as the clams, scallops, oysters, and their relatives, present a wide variety of forms showing generating curves. They differ from the univalves in having two conjugate spirals, the two axes of which have a definite relation to one another and some freedom of rotatory movement relative to one another (pl. 85).

The curve is simply expressed as the outline of the bivalve shell. It is commonly a plane curve, but it may be interrupted by interlocking valves or by valves of differing sizes. This curve may take several forms, including circular, elliptical, and triangular outlines.

The shell of the Chambered Nautilus, a cephalopod mollusk, has successive chambers that are secondarily subdivided by internal septa which serve to connect the chambers. The nautiloid shell grows as a continuous tube composed of separate chambers in the form of a logarithmic spiral (pl. 82). The animal occupies the outermost chamber.

81
Opeatostoma pseudodon Burrow (14–8) ▶

82
▲ *Nautilus pompilius* Linné (36–1)

83
Tonna melanostoma Jay (12–10 a) ▶

84
Polinices duplicatus Say
(11–4) ▲

84
◄ Operculum, *Turbo marmoratus* Linné (3–22a)

85
Glossus vulgaris Reeve (29–3)

86
Mitra stictica Link (15–7) ▲
Epitonium scalare Linné (7–1) ▼

Macron aethiops Reeve (14–1) ▲
Cassis cornuta Linné (12–1) ▼

87
Fasciolaria hunteria Perry (14–5) ▲
Harpa costata Linné (15–12) ▼

Cochlespira elegans Dall (16–6) ▲
Busycon contrarium Conrad (14–2) ▼

88
◄ *Cymbium olla* Linné (15–27)

89
Cymbium pepo Lightfoot (15–28) ▲

90
▲ *Thatcheria mirabilis* Sowerby (16–7)

91
Trophon geversianus Pallas (13–32) ▶

92
Harpa major Röding (15–11) ▶

93
Architectonica perspectivum Linné (6–2) ▶

94
Polinices duplicatus Say (11–4) ▲

95
Epitonium scalare Linné (7–1) ▶

VI.
The Color of Shells

Generally speaking, the most colorful seashells occur in shallow tropical waters. Temperate seas support less brightly colored species, and the polar seas are populated with species having largely whitish or pale-colored shells. Shell color appears, therefore, to be a reflection of water temperatures for the mollusks that inhabit the shallow water of the continental shelf. The shells of the most highly colored mollusks are commonly found in the warm waters of the mid latitudes, whereas the least brightly colored species occur in frigid waters of the high latitudes. Some species with brightly colored shells, however, live in deep, cold waters in the depths of the oceans. In marine mollusks, shell color ranges through all bands of the spectrum from red to violet, but bright greens and vivid blues are rarely seen in seashells. Various shades of brown and green, together with white, are the commonest colors. Large gaps remain in our knowledge of the chemical nature of shell pigmentation. While the shell can be deposited by the mantle of the mollusk throughout life, the pigments may be produced intermittently with the resulting color patterns characterizing the various species.

Pigments are thought to be deposited in the shells of some snails as a means of disposing of unmanageable waste products, especially excretory. In other gastropods, the color of the shell may also play a role in adaptation of environmental conditions, for example, in mimicry and protective coloration, but generally there is little direct evidence to support this assumption. The shells of some of the most colorful mollusks are covered in life by the fleshy mantle, as in the case of cowrie shells, or by the periostracum, or outer "skin," which protects the colorful shell, as in many of the cone shells. The brightly colored aperture or inner surface may be concealed by the soft parts, as in the case of the abalone shells, or by the large horny or limy operculum, as in most marine snails. Furthermore, many of the highly colored tropical species remain secreted during the day and are active only at night. Other colorful species live at depths below the penetration of light, and thus live in the dark. For these, the presence of a vividly colored shell would seem not to have a useful purpose.

Pigments of many types are distributed to the body of the mollusk by the blood system in the form of

◀ *Tonna luteostoma* Küster (12–10 b)

color-depositing cells. Those pigments that concentrate along the edge of the mollusk's mantle produce the varied colored patterns of the shell. Among the common pigments are the yellow to orange carotenoids, the tan to black melanins, the reddish porphyrins, the blue to red indigos, and the blue bilen.

Although it is generally believed that the color of shells represents food residues, these may be only one of several sources for molluscan pigments. Variation of the chemical composition and thermal changes of the water are thought also to influence the intensity or shade of color. Investigations, however, on the diet of abalone and top shells suggest that variation of shell coloration is related to food. Recent studies on the Red Abalone (pl. 119) disclosed that restricting animals to a diet of red algae resulted in a deep red color band being added to the shell, whereas those fed only on brown algae produced green-white or brown-white bands. Similar dietary studies on Japanese Top Shells also showed that color patterns are food-related. In a study of the variably colored Atlantic Dogwinkle, a muricid gastropod, darker color bands were said to result from feeding on blue sea mussels and lighter colors from eating barnacles. The pink shell of a species of limpet is thought to result from the ingestion of pink coralline algae by this species. In most species of mollusks, however, the variation of food types has not been demonstrated to be a factor in the production of shell coloration.

Color also may result from light refraction on the physical structure of the shells. For example, the brilliant iridescent coloration of the interior of abalone shells (pl. 106) and top shells is produced by the alternation of the wave length of light when the entering and reflected rays pass through the different layers of calcite. This nacreous layer, which is commonly known as mother-of-pearl, is used for inlays in jewelry and other ornaments.

Hybridization in marine mollusks apparently is a rare phenomenon in nature. In these instances, the hybrid shell may have some of the color characteristics of both parents. A few cases of hybridization are reported for abalones, cowries, true oysters, pearl oysters, hard-shell clams, and tellins. A recent investigation of west American abalones resulted in the recognition of twelve hybrid crosses among six of the eight species living in the region. Artificial discoloration of the molluscan shell may result from adverse growing conditions. The abnormal coloration is not inherited by the offspring of the affected individuals when they live in normal environments. The melanistic forms of some species of cowrie shells may be caused by pathogens.

Shell Ornamentation: A Mysterious Code

Although man has collected and admired colorful shells for centuries, he is still largely baffled by the complex biological system that controls the deposition of color and sculptural ornamentation in these creatures. With the exception of those species with shells exhibiting obvious adaptive coloration such as camouflage or mimicry, there is no apparent correlation with environmental factors for most species, including many with shells having intricate color ornamentation. The presence of coloration in the shell does provide us with certain information concerning the biology of each species. It is this biological "code," preserved in the molluscan shell

96. Spotted Tun Shell (12–10b)
97. Panamic Thorny Oyster (25–10)
98. American Thorny Oyster (25–11)
99. Greenish Cap Limpet (2–7)
100 left. Lettered Cone (16–11)
100 center. Betuline Cone (16–28)
100 right. Marbled Cone (16–8)
101 top left. Weasel Cone (16–14)
101 top center. Courtly Cone (16–21)
101 top right. Fig Cone (16–27)
101 middle left. Textile Cone (16–23)
101 center. Episcopal Cone (16–22)
101 middle right. Captain's Cone (16–15)
101 bottom left. Chestnut Cone (16–33)
101 bottom left center. Bubble Cone (16–30)
101 bottom right center. Prelate Cone (16–25)
101 bottom right. Maldive Cone, color phase (16–19)
102. Ducal Thorny Oyster (25–13)
103. Fluted Giant Clam (29–5)

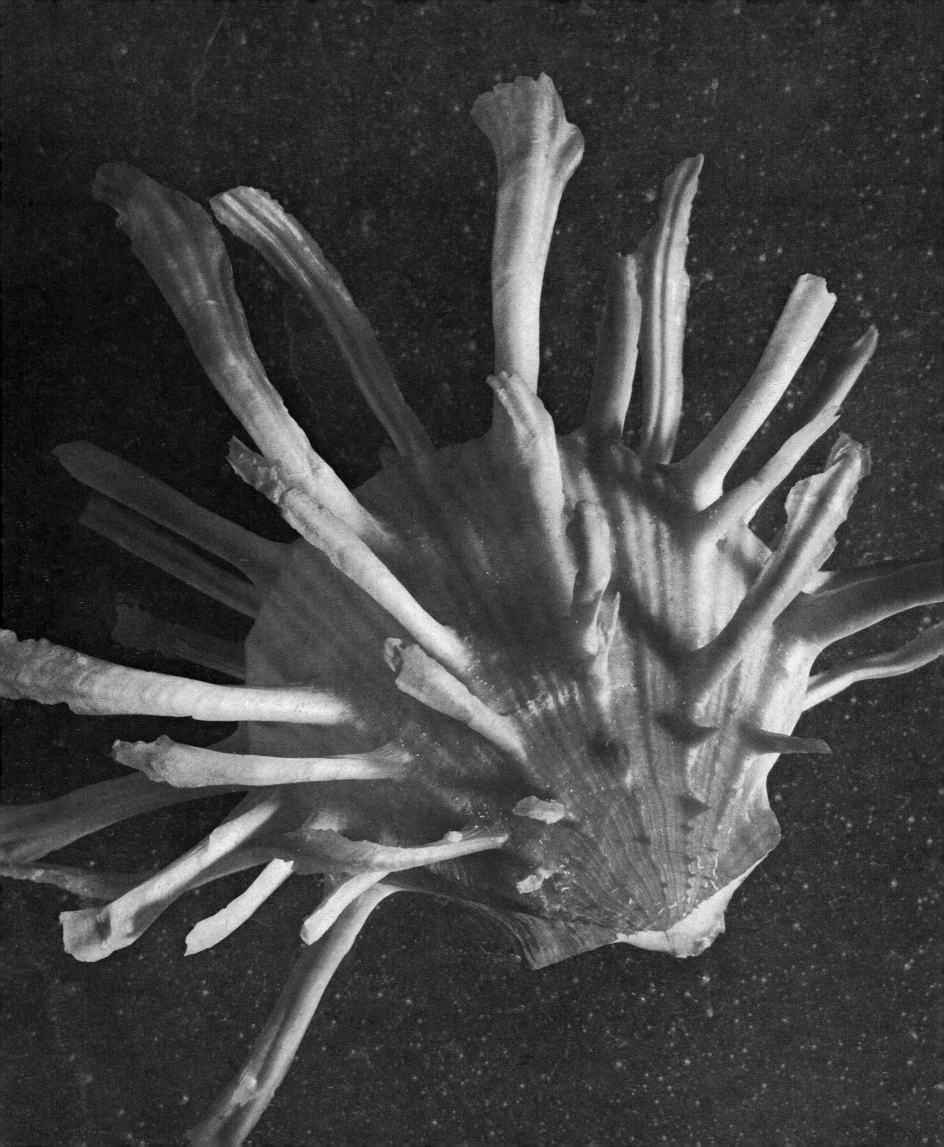

98
◀ *Spondylus americanus* Hermann (25–11)

99
Acmaea viridula Lamarck (2–7) ▲

100

▲ *Conus litteratus* Linné (16–11), left
Conus betulinus Linné (16–28), center
Conus marmoreus Linné (16–8), right

101 top left to right
Conus maldivus Hwass (16–19)
Conus aulicus Linné (16–21)
Conus figulinus Linné (16–27)
center left to right
Conus textile Linné (16–23)
Conus episcopus Hwass (16–22)

Conus capitaneus Linné (16–15)
bottom left to right
Conus coccineus Gmelin (16–33)
Conus bullatus Linné (16–30)
Conus praelatus Hwass (16–25)
Conus maldivus Hwass (16–19) ▶

Spondylus ducalis Röding (25–13) ▲

Tridacna maximus Röding (29–5) ▶

as color patterns and sculptural features, that we must attempt to decipher. Fortunately, some color patterns and most sculptural features of the shell may be preserved in the extinct ancestors of the living species, and these fossils serve to provide a clue to the evolutionary traits of most of the molluscan groups.

After we determine the range of variables exhibited by the shell, including such factors as shape, size, sculpture, pigment intensity, and temporal persistence of ornamentation, we can attempt to decipher the perplexing biological code displayed by the molluscan shell. These observations suggest that the various kinds of pigment and sculptural ornamentation result from different methods of shell deposition. Spiral bands and ribs are produced by continuous production in a spiral direction of pigment or sculpture by spatially localized cell groups of the mantle edge, and axial lines and ribs are produced by the discontinuous production of pigment or sculpture along the entire mantle edge. Checks, blotches, and spots are the result of various combinations of these methods in which production of the pigment-producing centers is not continuous both temporally and spatially. Thus we find that the interruption in the deposition of the pigment pattern, together with discontinuous deposition of the sculptural features, serves to produce the vast array of design and architecture seen in the molluscan shell. Most of these features appear to be genetically controlled, and they are basic inheritable characters of species. Some, as we have seen, may be influenced by environmental factors. Recent investigations of the biochemistry, physiology, and ecology of mollusks indicate that we have much to learn before we can unravel the biological secrets of the code.

The rate of growth is known to influence, in large part, the character of the shell coloration. Rapid growth results generally in more base color relative to localized color pattern, while slower growth permits the production of more extensive shell patterns, with the result that the shell may be dark colored. Diversity in shell ornamentation is further produced by a wide range in the intensity of pigmentation and by varying degrees of development in sculptural features.

In some intertidal species, growth proceeds in a 24-hour rhythmic cycle. In these gastropods, a new spiral growth line and associated sculptural nodes and pigment spots are added to the apertural edge of the shell per day during the period of maximum growth. In most shallow-water species, however, shell production does not correspond to the 24-hour cycle. In these, the growth process may be related to a lunar or semilunar period resulting from the interaction of tidal and diel (light intensity) influences which apparently trigger the rhythmic activity. Although some kind of an environmental stimulus may be required to synchronize the onset of the growth rhythm in these species, the nature of these mechanisms and the interaction of this cycle with other inherited rhythms is not understood.

Few marine mollusks have been raised experimentally under conditions duplicating their natural environment. Therefore, it is difficult to determine the features of the ornamentation which are inheritable and in what ways these features are influenced directly or indirectly by the environment in which the mollusk lives. Such investigations are direly needed before we can expand our meager knowledge of this subject. We know, however, that apertural varices are not produced in some gastropods, such as *Strombus,* until the shell has attained maximum size, presumably when the animal has reached sexual maturity. Furthermore, the regularity of the deposition of varices in others, for example *Murex,* would appear to be an inherent character which is independent of environmental factors other than suitable hydroclimatic conditions.

The available information suggests that the adaptive significance of shell ornamentation is probably indirect. The ornamentation apparently is the result of the interaction of several biochemical and physiological rhythms in which selection may actually be acting on several biological characters rather than on shell ornamentation alone. Certain rhythms of activity, such as spawning, feeding, and oxygen consumption, are obviously adaptive, for they may be correlated with tidal and diel cycles in some intertidal species. Environmental factors that appear to have a major effect on the development of shell color and patterns of ornamentation include temperature, light, submergence, and perhaps oxygen. Therefore, shell ornamentation is a reflection of a multitude of biochemical activities within the animal and of critical environmental influences acting on the animal to produce in the shell a record of its life history. This biological code hopefully will be deciphered as we accumulate more information on the relationship of the respective roles played by inherited and environmental factors in producing shell ornamentation.

Fluorescence in Seashells

When some molluscan shells are exposed to long-wave ultraviolet radiations, a red fluorescence is emitted. Chemical analysis of the pigments of these shells demonstrates that this emission is due to the presence of a porphyrin, which has been termed conchoporphyrin. The chemical complex of these acid-soluble pigments is intermediate in character between coproporphyrin, and uroporphyrin, which are derived from fecal and urinary waste products respectively. Uroporphyrins have also been isolated from some molluscan shells, including the keyhole limpets and top shells.

Two reddish shades of porphyrin emission, a vivid scarlet and a weaker pink, are commonly produced under ultraviolet light. Other apparently pigment-related colors of fluorescence, generally of a low intensity, have been detected. A nacreous shell generally fluoresces blue, while bivalve adductor scars emit a white or yellow light. Some specimens of cowries, for example Tiger Cowries, exhibit orange emision. The concentration of porphyrin in individual specimens of a sample may vary greatly, from those with large amounts to those without a trace. Therefore, a large series of specimens must be examined before excluding the possible presence of porphyrin in a given species.

Porphyrin deposition, producing either scarlet or pink fluorescence, is known to occur in modern species referable to the following groups: (1) gastropods – abalones, keyhole limpets, top shells, star shells, pheasant shells, nerites, sundials, cowries, trivias, eratos, margin shells, and several opisthobranchs, including notably the bubble shells; (2) bivalves – pearl oysters, wing oysters, hammer oysters, saddle oysters, and a few other families. Traces of pink fluorescence have been detected in some scaphopods (pl. 107) and chitons (pl. 114). Fluorescence also can be activated in certain fossil shells, including some lacking visible shell pigment, to enable the visual reconstruction of the original ornamentation of the specimens. In this way these fossils can be compared with their surviving descendants.

The deposition of porphyrin in the molluscan shell appears to be most common in the primitive marine gastropods, in certain of the opisthobranchs, and in several kinds of oysters, although it is not present in all these groups nor in all species of any one family. The trivias and eratos, close relatives of the cowries, represent an isolated group of the higher gastropods with a high degree of incidence of this pigment. In the few species of cowries involved, the porphyrin apparently is associated with pigments deposited after the formation of the mature lip. The Map Cowrie (pl. 175) presents a good example of this pattern of emission, for the base of the shell may emit a striking scarlet pattern when exposed to ultraviolet radiation. Fluorescence is generally most evident in small examples of a species, suggesting that dilution by shell matter takes place as the individual matures.

These often beautiful patterns of fluorescence can be photographed in a darkroom by using a very fast film and a special yellow lens filter, for example Wratten No. 8, K.2. Long-wave ultraviolet lamps of 3200 to 4000 angstrom units are recommended for this purpose.

Porphyrin fluorescence of the molluscan shell should not be confused with bioluminescence, the production of light by living organisms. Luminescent light production is an oxidative reaction result-

106
▲ *Haliotis fulgens* Philippi (1–2)

107 left
Dentalium formosum Adams and Reeve (21–2) ▶
107 right
Dentalium elephantinum Linné (21–1) ▶

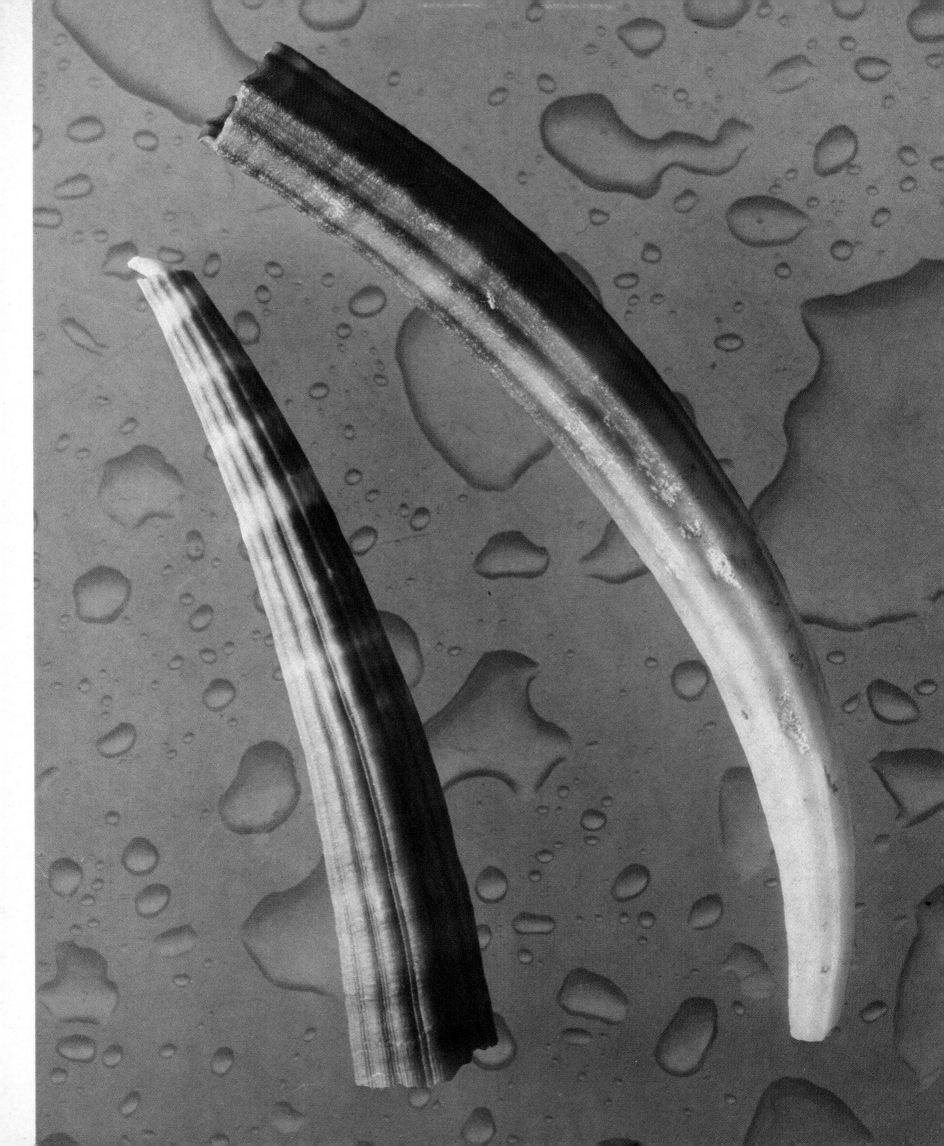

108
Spondylus gaederopus Linné (25–9)

109
Tectus pyramis Born (3–7)

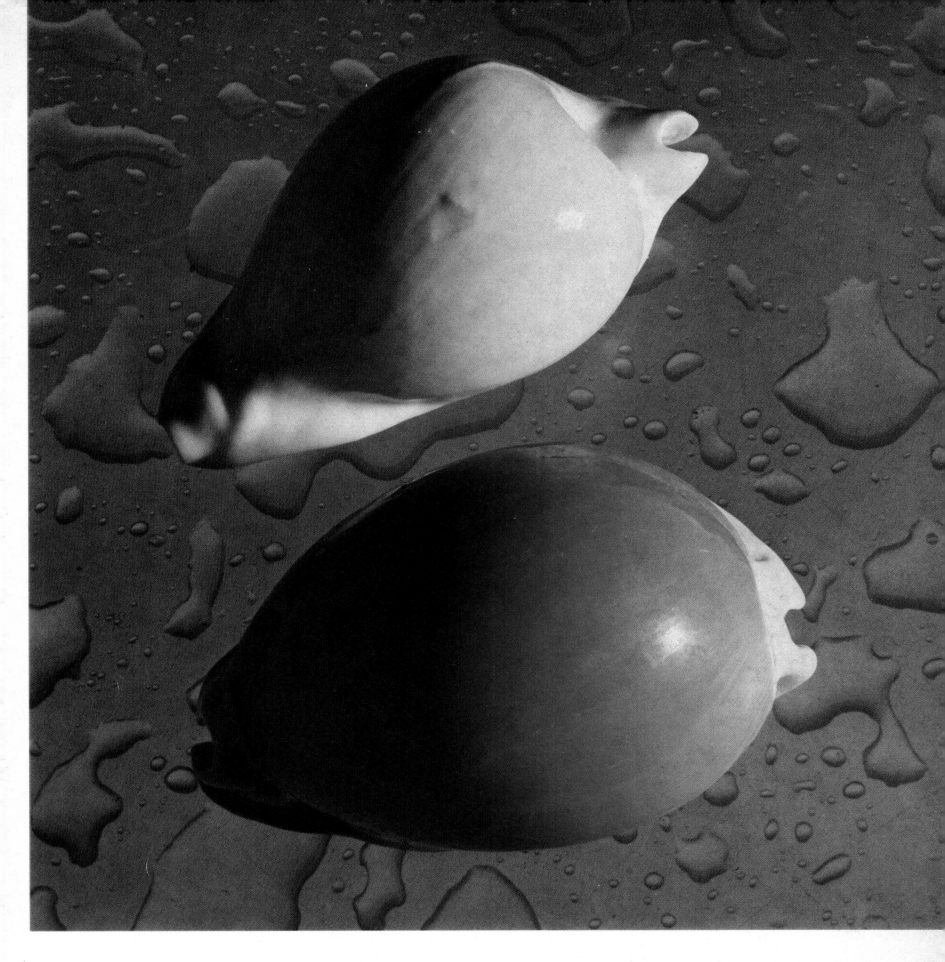

ing from the decay of a light-emitting molecule brought to the excited state by a chemical-enzyme reaction. Bioluminescence is common in organisms living in the oceans, including some deep-sea squids and a few other pelagic mollusks, which are capable of producing brilliant displays of "phosphorescence."

The presence of porphyrins in the molluscan shell does not appear to be directly related to specialized adaptations or to nutritional requirements, although they may be secreted, as we have noted, with the shell as a means of disposal of metabolic waste products. Therefore, interesting biological questions are raised concerning the ability of some molluscan groups to produce and deposit porphyrins. Extensive biochemical and physiological investigations on this subject are needed before we

can hope to understand better this natural phenomenon.

The Violet Snails: The Armada Builders

Among the seashells collectors sometimes find in great numbers washed ashore from warm waters in all parts of the world are the pelagic violet snails of of the genus *Janthina* (pl. 120). These gastropods are unusual in several ways. Firstly, their shells and bodies are a beautiful bluish purple, a color not frequently encountered in seashells. Secondly, these fragile mollusks are adapted to a life of floating passively on the surface of the sea. They construct a raft of air-filled mucous floats to which they cling by the foot in an upside-down position. Large num-

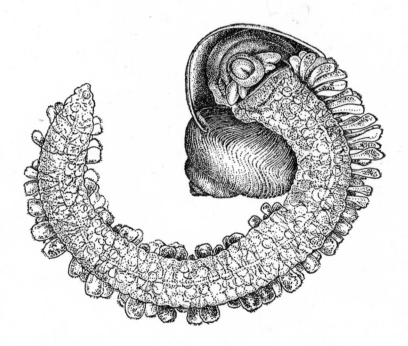

A violet snail (*Janthina exigua* Lamarck) as seen from above in floating position with its foot attached to the raft. (After D. Laursen, 1953)

bers of these snails may join their rafts together to form a huge floating armada composed of thousands of individuals. Occasionally storms or currents carry the rafts ashore and deposit the helpless snails on beaches, where they expire, for they are not able to crawl back into the water. A small crab, the same color as the violet snails, may be found inhabiting the rafts, living with the snails in a symbiotic association.

The beautiful, wide-ranging violet snails have long held the interest of naturalists owing to their unusual color and peculiar habits. They were first described and figured in a treatise published in Rome by Fabius Columna in 1616. In the course of time, scientists have applied more than sixty different scientific names to the living species comprising the genus. This multitude of names was reduced to five valid species in the most recent monographic study of *Janthina*. These snails occur most commonly in tropical and subtropicial seas, but shells occasionally drift ashore from colder waters, including those of the British Isles and New Zealand. It seems unlikely that these animals are able to propagate in the cooler boreal regions.

Although the shell looks like a typical gastropod, the specialized living habits of these snails has caused them to be classified with many different kinds of marine snails. They are now placed near the wentletraps in the superfamily Epitoniacea rather than with other groups of pelagic snails. It is interesting to note that the violet snails have in common with the wentletraps a cleftlike radula divided into two equal parts and that both of these snails feed largely on coelenterates. The wentletraps commonly feed on sea anemones and other attached coelenterates, whereas the violet snails frequently eat pelagic coelenterates, such as jellyfish. It is not certain whether this relationship reflects a common ancestor for these groups of snails or represents adaptation to similar food preferences by diverse families of predacious, carnivorous gastropods. It appears likely, however, that the violet snails took to pelagic life early in their evolutionary history.

The violet snails have no eyes and no powers of directive swimming, and they can feed only when by chance they drift against another pelagic organism such as the Portuguese man-of-war. The snails have been observed to abandon the float when feeding and to crawl on the underside of the coelenterates. They exude a purple dye, which may anesthetize the stinging cells in the tentacles of the coelenterates, before feeding with the radula. Like the violet snails, many wentletraps secrete a purple dye, which may serve as an anesthetic when they feed on sea anemones.

The violet snails are protandric hermaphrodites; that is, the gonads first produce sperm in the male phase and later produce eggs in the female phase. The male lacks a copulatory organ. The mobile sperm cells are transplanted by a large featherlike carrier to the oviduct of the female. Some species deposit egg capsules on the underside of the float. In others, including the Common Violet Snail, the eggs are incubated and hatched within the body of the female. The young are born as free-swimming veligers.

On the celebrated exploratory voyage of the *Endeavour* under the command of James Cook, the naturalist Joseph Banks netted specimens of violet snails while sailing well out in the Atlantic. Banks recorded in his journal the following observations, dated October 7, 1768, regarding these pelagic mollusks: "They are found floating on top of the water by means of a small cluster of Bubbles filled with air, which are composed of a tenacious slimey substance, not easily parting with its contents; these keep him suspended on the surface of the water and serve as a hiding for his Eggs, and it is probable that he never goes to the bottom, or willingly comes near any shore, as his shell is of so brittle construction

◀ *Mopalia hindsi* Sowerby (20–1) top
Mopalia ciliata Sowerby (20–2) right
Mopalia muscosa Gould, interior and exterior (20–3) center
Chiton stokesii Broderip (20–5) bottom

Acanthopleura echinata Barnes (20–4) ▲

116
▲ *Turbo speciosus* Reeve (3–20)

117
Turbo reevei Philippi (3–18) ▶

118
Hexaplex cichoreus Gmelin (13–13)

119
Haliotis rufescens Swainson (1–2 a)

that few fresh water snails are so thin. Every shell contains within it about a teaspoonful of Liquid, which it easily discharges on being touched, this is of a most beautiful red purple colour and easily dies linnen clothes; it may be well worth inquiry whether or not this is the *purpura* of the ancients as the shell is certainly found in the Mediterranean. We have not yet taken a sufficient quantity of the Shells to try the experiment, probably we shall do so soon." (The *Endeavour* Journal of Joseph Banks, 1768–1771, ed. J. C. Beaglehole, vol. 1, p.

171, 1962.) We now know that the Dye Murex was the primary source of the royal tyrian purple first used by the Phoenicians and later by the Greeks, Romans, and the early Christians to dye wool and cotton cloth.

These remarkable animals, the armada-builders of the molluscan world, have been reported to form groups of drifting rafts in the Atlantic Ocean extending nearly two hundred nautical miles long, and one of these shoals sighted off the coast of Florida was recorded to be ninety miles wide.

120 bottom left
◀ *Janthina janthina* Linné (7–3)
120 bottom right
Coralliophila violacea Kiener (13–52)

120 top
◀ *Haliotis cracherodii* Leach (1–2 b)

122 top
Chlamys muscosus Wood (25–7)

122 bottom
Mytilus viridis Linné (24–1)

123 center
Chlamys nobilis Reeve (25–3)

123 left
Chlamys asperrimus Lamarck (25–4)

123 right
Chlamys bifrons Lamarck (25–6)

◄
124 top
Pecten ziczac Linné (25–8)
124 bottom
Lyropecten nodosus Linné (25–2)

Spondylus americanus Hermann (25–11) ▲

126
▲ *Lambis chiragra* Linné (9–17)

127 left
Aulica aulica Lightfoot (15–16) ▶
127 right
Cymbiolacca complexa Iredale (15–19) ▶

VII.
The Surface Texture of Shells

The outer surface of shells may appear to the unaided eye to be smooth. However, with the aid of magnification even the smoothest-looking shell is seen to be delicately sculptured, often in a most artistic and appealing manner. In gastropods the growth lines parallel the outer lip of the aperture and run at right angles to the sutures, as exhibited in the White Galeodea (pl. 137 bottom right). In bivalves they parallel the margins of the two valves, as seen in the ribbing of the Elegant Disk Clam (pl. 131). Periods of interrupted growth may be indicated by prominent breaks in the sculptural pattern, as exemplified on the body whorl of the Magnificent Wentletrap shown in plate 134. In some gastropod groups, for example the rock shells, frog shells, and tritons, the period of arrested growth is marked by a pronounced thickening of the outer lip, which is termed a varix, as shown in the Gem Triton (pl. 140 bottom left). The surface of the gastropod shell is not infrequently also sculptured with ridges, grooves, ribs, tubercles, or other kinds of projections that parallel the sutures or run at right angles to them. Various examples of these structural modifications are depicted in this chapter.

The bivalves exhibit less variety in surface ornamentation, although some possess raised ribs, which may be variously modified in the form of scales or plications. For example, the Lion's Paw (pl. 133 top right) and the Plicate Venus (p. 132), and others may have spines or other projections of varying kinds, which are discussed in chapter VIII.

In life, the surface sculpture of clams and snails is commonly covered by a protective outer layer, the periostracum. This outer "skin" may be eroded off part of the surface in old specimens—see, for example, the specimen of Twisted Ark pictured here in plate 138. In such cases, the outer limy layers of the shell are frequently also eroded.

The surface of shells often serves as a base of attachment for sessile invertebrates and for seaweeds. Oyster spat and serpulid worm tubes are shown attached to the surface of a scallop shell (pl. 142), and similar worm tubes appear on the Winged Tree-Oyster (pl. 139). Such organisms generally do not interfere with the normal life processes of the host species, although some burrowing organisms, often other species of mollusks, may cause the death of the host mollusk in cases of extreme infestations.

◀ 128 left to right
Ancilla velesiana Iredale (15–2)
Ancilla albocallosa Lischke (15–1)
Mitra mitra Linné (15–6)
Vexillum vittatum Swainson (15–10)

Spiny oysters, chamas, and others that have the lower valve cemented to hard substrates such as rocks, stony corals, and wood may take the shape of the object to which they are attached. Those specimens living on smooth surfaces tend to have a flat shell, while those affixed to coral or other irregular surfaces become uneven in shape. The sculptural form of the base on which the bivalve is attached is sometimes duplicated on both valves when the growing edge of the upper valve rests on the irregular surface of the base. The valves of mangrove oysters frequently exhibit a central rib formed after the shape of the tree branch to which they are attached, but oysters of the same species living on the smooth trunk of the mangrove tree lack such a rib.

The shells of mollusks that live on the surface of other shells may be modified according to the sculptural features possessed by the host shell. This condition is not uncommonly found in slipper shells, limpetlike gastropods with a strong, muscular foot. Those slipper snails that are attached to ribbed bivalves such as scallops have a ribbed shell, while those living on smooth shells have a smooth surface. Specimens that have lived at different times on both kinds of surfaces may have a shell exhibiting both sculptural features. These morphological changes are also common to the jingle shells, which are bivalves.

The physical environment can also play a selective role in the development of surface sculpture. The common Dogwinkle, a thaid gastropod related to murex shells, serves well to demonstrate this observation. Specimens living in shallow, highly turbulent waters generally have less spiny shells than those from deeper, quieter waters. Furthermore, those living in very exposed habitats may have stunted, short spired, thick shells with large apertures, presumably adaptive characters which reduce the resistance to wave shock. On the other hand, sheltered areas, such as estuaries and protected straits and coasts, support populations of thaid snails usually with larger, thinner shells, which are often higher spired and have smaller apertures than those living in exposed habitats.

The surface of the gastropod and pelecypod shell may be dull, but in many mollusks the shell has a high luster, especially in the apertural region of certain gastropods that possess a prominent parietal callus on the columellar lip. In other species, such as the cowries, which have the dorsum of the shell covered by the mantle, a high luster is also produced. The natural luster may be dulled by erosion in old specimens or in diseased individuals.

129
Ficus dussumieri Valenciennes (12–11)

130
Acanthina muricata Broderip (13–35) ▲

131
Dosinia elegans Conrad (30–4) ▶

132
◀ *Circomphalus plicata*
Gmelin (30–1)

133
▲ *Concholepas concholepas* Bruguière (13–42)
Placuna sella Linné (26–1) ▼

133
Lyropecten nodosus Linné (25–2) ▲
Concholepas concholepas Bruguière (13–42) ▼

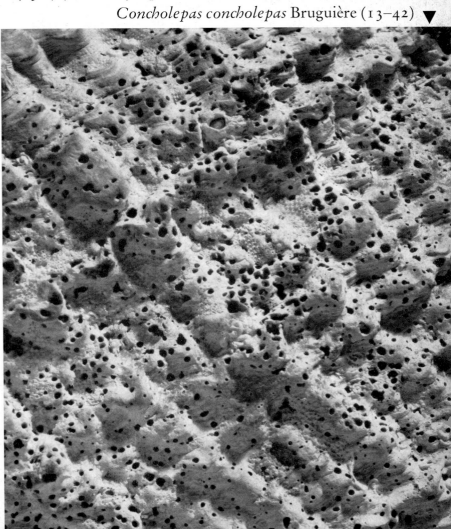

◀ *Amaea magnifica* Sowerby (7–2)

Astralium calcar Linné (3–14) ▲

136
Harpa costata Linné (15–12)

137
▲ *Acanthina muricata* Broderip (13–35)
▼ *Tonna melanostoma* Jay (12–10a)

137
Phalium granulatum Born (12–5) ▲
Galeodea leucodoma Dall (12–6) ▼

138
◄ *Trisidos tortuosa* Linné (22–1)

139
Isognomon isognomon Linné (23–1) ▲

140
▲ *Turritella terebra* Linné (6–1)
▼ *Cymatium rubeculum* Linné (12–8)

140
Gemmula congener cosmoi Sykes (16–3) ▲
Conus sulcatus Hwass (16–34) ▼

141
▲ *Turritella duplicata* Linné (6–1 a)

▼ *Nerita textilis* Gmelin (4–1)

141
Thais kiosquiformis Duclos (13–40) ▲

Strombus vomer iredalei Abbott (9–15) ▼

◄ *Argopecten irradians* Lamarck (25–00)

▲ *Chione gnidia* Broderip and Sowerby (30–6)

VIII.
Knobs and Spines

As we have noted elsewhere in this discussion, the various forms of ornamentation on the exterior surface of the shell, the striae, ribs, nodules, imbrications, and spines, to mention the more common sculptural forms, are produced by similar and corresponding irregularities in the surface conformation of the margin of the mantle and are secreted by the outer, growing edge of the mantle.

In gastropods all of the sculptural features are originally deposited at the edge of the apertural lip where new material is added to the shell. The spines are first formed as thornlike hollow tubes, which may be channeled on the apertural side of the shell in the case of snails. The spines in some species, for example those of the Great Stag Antler Murex (pl. 155), become filled with solid shell matter as the growing edge of the mantle is withdrawn. In other species the mature spines retain open channels, as seen in the West Indian Murex (pl. 158). Knoblike sculptural projections are formed in a similar manner by the mantle but are closed when completely formed, as exemplified by the Knobbed Purple (pl. 152).

In bivalves the new shell material is deposited by the mantle along the outer margins of the two valves. As most bivalves live buried in soft substrates – sand, mud, and ooze – this mode of life largely restricts the development of spinose surface ornamentation. Prominent spines are produced, however, in the Panamic Comb Venus (pl. 149 bottom), but they are restricted to the posterior end of the valves. In bivalves that attach to hard substrates above the sea bottom, prominent spines may be developed. For example, the Long-spined Thorny Oyster (pl. 146) forms concentrically placed rows of spines of varying lengths.

Although the purpose of spines and similar forms of ornamentation of the molluscan shell is often said to be protection from attacks of predators, a satisfactory explanation of the evolutionary significance of these sculptural elaborations has not been ascertained. There are instances, for example, in which we find a species with extreme spinosity, such as the Venus Comb Murex (pl. 145), living together with a closely related species of Murex that lacks well-developed spines. Obviously, the spineless forms have successfully adapted to the same environmental conditions as species with well-developed spines. Perhaps the various types of sculptural modifications developed in the shells reflect, in part, adaptations to the requirements of locomotion by the mollusks, including the need for stability in motion and gravitational resistance. At the present time, we can only speculate on the purpose, if any, served by the possession of elaborate surface ornamentation in most species of snails and clams.

In some of the thaid snails, however, the shell has a long, thornlike tooth on the outer lip that the animal uses as a wedge in preventing closure of the plates of barnacles or the valves of the clams on which the gastropod preys. A similar projected toothlike structure is formed by the Zebra Thorn-Shell (pl. 156 top right), a species classified with the Tulip Snails. The purpose of this spine, the largest apertural tooth developed in any living gastropod, is not known, but it may also serve for wedging apart the valves of clams in order to facilitate the devouring of its prey.

The spines are commonly the same color as the rest of the shell. Among the most beautiful shells, however, are those with spines of darker pigmentation than the body of the shell. The Great Stag-antler Murex (pl. 155) frequently has a tan shell ornamented with chocolate spines, and the shell of the Chicory Murex (pl. 154) may be white with brown or black spines. Many specimens of Spiny Oysters have a white shell with spines of lavender, yellow, orange, or red, or the spines may be white and the shell variously colored.

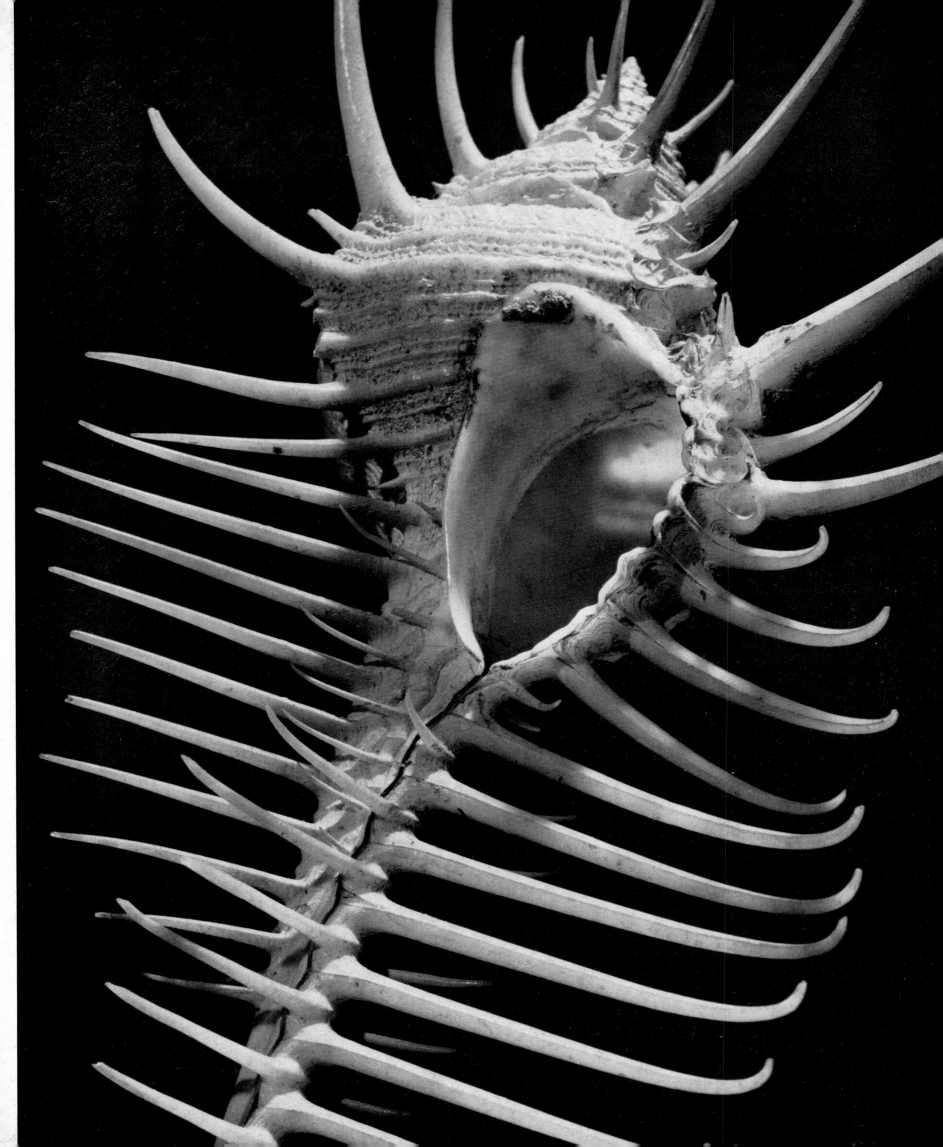

146
▲ *Spondylus wrightianus* Crosse (25–12)

147
Murex cervicornis Lamarck (13–11) ▶

148
▲ *Lambis lambis* Linné
(9–19)

148
◄ *Acanthocardia aculeata*
Linné (29–1)

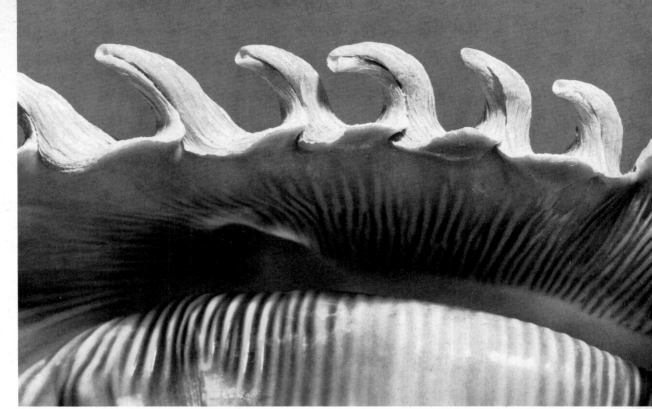

▲ *Homalocantha zamboi* Burch (13–23)

Chicoreus palmarosae Lamarck (13–15) ▶

153
Melongena corona
Gmelin (14–4) ▶

152
▲ *Austrotrophon*
catalinensis Oldroyd
(13–34)

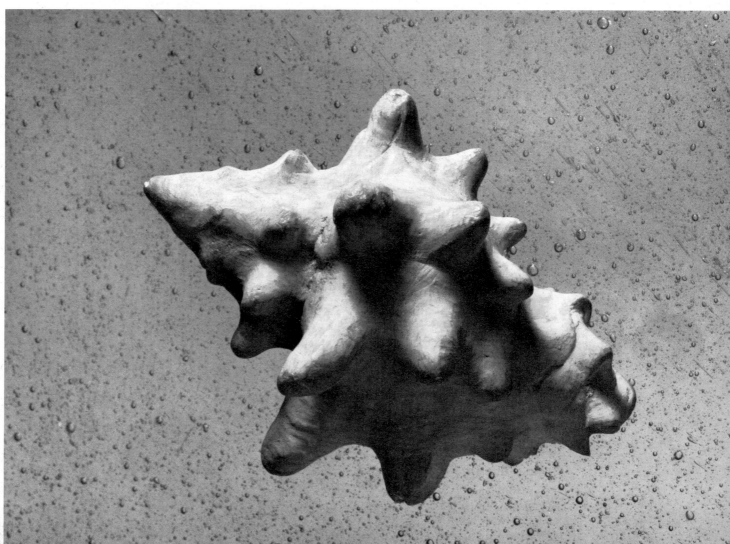

152
Thais armigera Link
(13–37) ▶

154
▲ *Hexaplex cichoreus* Gmelin (13–13)

155
Hexaplex cornucervi Röding (13–12) ▶

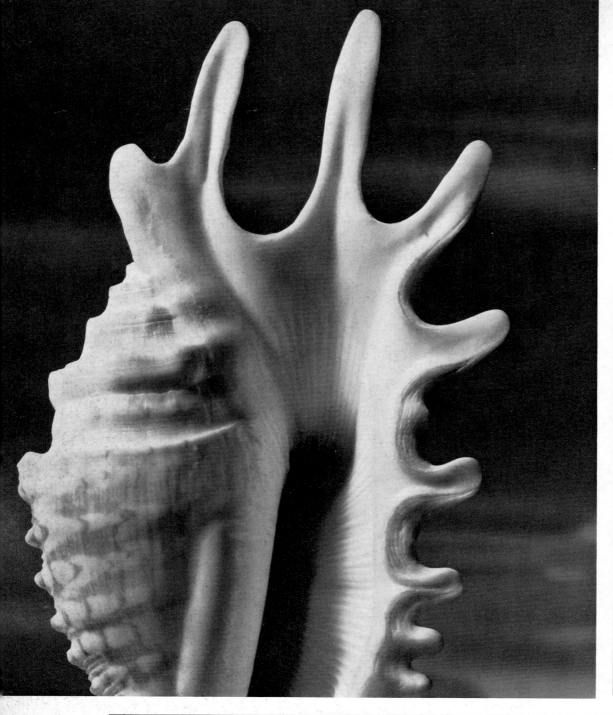

156
◀ *Lambis violacea* Swainson (9–22)

156
▲ *Opeatostoma pseudodon*
Burrow (14–8)

156
◀ *Chicoreus dilectus* A. Adams
(13–18)

157
Murex cornutus Linné
(13–9) ▶

158
▲ *Chicoreus brevifrons* Lamarck (13–17)

159
Thais haemastoma Linné (13–39) ▶

IX.
Ornamental Design

The presence of artistic color patterns adds immensely to our aesthetic appreciation of the varied shapes and sculpture of the molluscan shell. Although many shells are monochromatic (one-colored), the shells of most species are polychromatic (multicolored). Color banding is common, as are a variety of color patterns composed of dots, stripes, circles, triangles, rectangles, chevrons, and wavy lines. Some of the intricate color patterns appear to be arranged in almost a mathematically precise manner, although the shells of no two individuals are exactly the same. The patterns may change as the mollusk grows, and the juveniles of the species may differ in appearance from the adult. In some species of gastropods the color patterns are absent from the early whorls, or may be restricted to the body whorl. In bivalves the color designs may be lacking on the region of the umbo but appear on the older parts of the shell.

The basic color designs of the shell, although highly variable in some species, appear to be limited by the range of pattern variation found in the genetic pool of the individuals composing the breeding population. As was noted in chapter VI, the external coloration of the shell is produced by pigment-depositing cells along the outer edge of the mollusk's mantle. The production of pigment may be intermittent, although the deposition of limy shell material may occur throughout the life of the mollusk.

If the color-depositing cells remain in the same position along the growing edge of the mantle and continuously supply pigment, a simple stripe will appear on the newly deposited shell. On the other hand, an oblique stripe will be produced if the cells of the color-producing centers secrete pigment alternately or move across the edge of the mantle. The placement and periods of secretion of the color cells apparently serve to determine the production of the various kinds of color patterns that appear in the newly deposited shell material.

The actual mechanics of the process of pattern formation in the molluscan shell is poorly understood. The following summary is deduced from observations made from examining the shells. It is not known, for instance, whether the color-secreting cells actually move from place to place in the mantle or whether secretion shifts from one group of cells to those in another site. Continuous secretion by color cells along the edge of the mantle would appear to produce radial lines, bands, zones, or homogeneously colored shells, depending on the duration of the process of pigment deposition in the newly formed shell material. If the motion of the mantle is constant, the expected results are straight, obliquely arranged lines or bands. An acceleration of motion would produce curves of various kinds, the regularity of which would be dependent on the rate of acceleration. Oscillatory motions appear to produce weakly expressed radial bands.

Intermittent pigment deposition, on the other hand, apparently results in the production of radial rows of spots, of lines, or less commonly, of concentric lines. As a consequence of intermittent deposition, rows of rectangles *en échelon* may be produced instead of oblique rows of parallelograms. In these instances, the movement of the color-producing cells to different sites in the mantle appears to take place between phases of secretion by the color cells rather than during the period of pigment deposition, or secretion of the pigment cells may cease in some sites and be activated in other areas. Deposition would not seem to be restricted to lateral movements, as the mantle may be directed outward and inward to form patterns, for example those deposited within the aperture of the gastropod shell.

In the cowries and their relatives, the entire surface of the mantle, which may completely cover the dorsum of the shell in life, is apparently involved in the process of shell deposition. In these colorful shells, the pigmentation cells appear to be arranged in a complex manner in order to produce the color patterns over a large area of the mantle. A remarkable variety of color patterns occurs in these shells, including circles in the Eyed Cowrie (pl. 174) and zigzag lines in the Map Cowrie (pl. 175).

Distinctive color patterns may occur in different groups of mollusks. The triangular tent pattern, for

◀ *Hydatina albocincta* van der Hoeven (17–1)

example, is characteristic of the Textile Cone (pl. 166 bottom), but these patterns also appear in the Tent Olive (pls. 162 and 163) and in several species of venerid bivalves, including the Chocolate Flamed Venus (pl. 167).

Color patterns may also vary considerably among individual specimens of the same species. The Zebra Volute, as the name suggests, may have a highly striped shell; but it may also have a shell with few or no stripes (pl. 172). A wide range of color patterns is exhibited by the Australian Pheasant Shell (pl. 173).

Color patterns may be altered by periods of interrupted growth, as evidenced by the specimen of Textile Cone shown with an irregular pattern near the bottom of the picture in plate 166 (bottom). Injury to the growing area of the shell may also result in the presence of an irregular color pattern after the shell has been repaired by the mantle of the mollusk. This condition is exemplified by the repaired axial line on the body whorl of the specimen of Striped Monodont pictured in plate 169 (top left).

A recent investigation of the food preferences of the predatory and highly venomous cone snails suggests there is a relationship between the kinds of food these gastropods eat and the basic color patterns of their shells. Of the fifty-five species of *Conus* from various parts of the world studied, it was found that 65 per cent were vermivores (worm eaters), 17 per cent were molluscivores (mollusk eaters) and 18 per cent piscivores (fish eaters). An analysis of the color patterns of the shells in terms of the different feeding types showed that the tent pattern (as in the Courtly Cone, pl. 165 top left) was present in all of the molluscivores, 10 per cent of the piscivores, and 2.7 per cent of the vermivores. The pattern of interrupted striae (as in the Striate Cone, pl. 165 bottom right) was found in all of the piscivores and 13.9 per cent of the vermivores and was totally absent in the molluscivores, for the species considered. From these findings it appears that tent markings are positively relevant to molluscivores, and the pattern of interrupted striae is similarly relevant to piscivores, whereas these color characters are mostly negative to the vermivores. Although neither of these color patterns is restricted to a single feeding type, each pattern is preponderant to one feeding type only. The results of this investigation, therefore, imply that food preferences may play a role as an adaptive factor in the evolution of the color patterns found in molluscan shells.

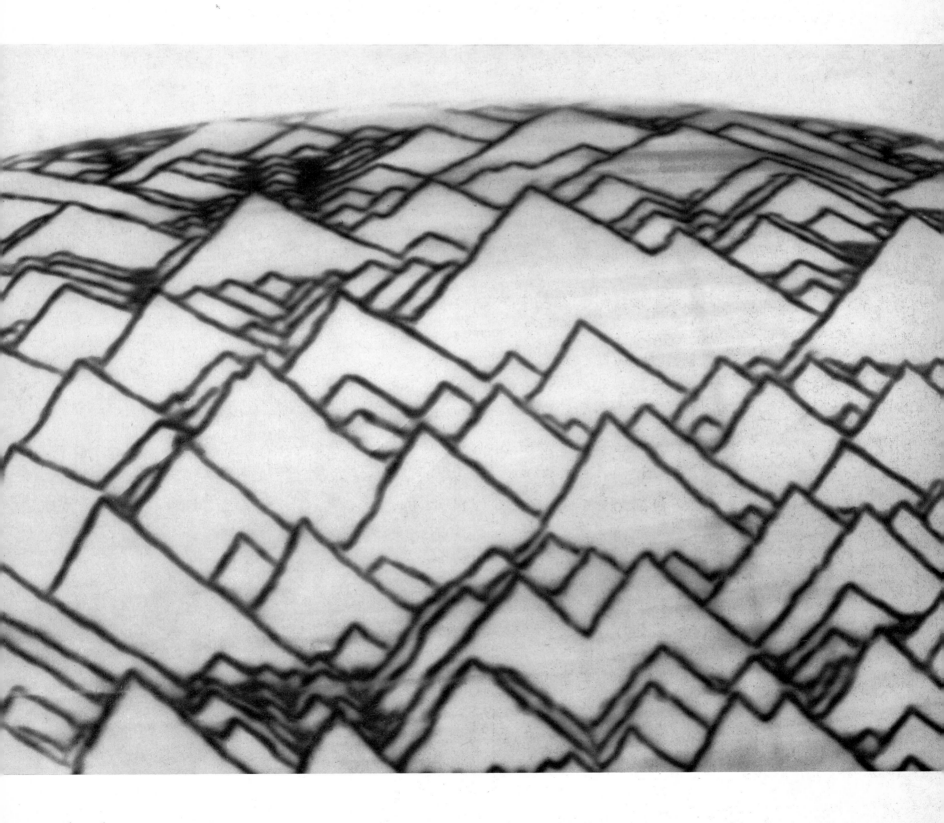

162, 163
◀ *Oliva porphyria* Linné (15–3) ▲

164

Conus genuanus Linné (16–29) ▲

Conus spurius Gmelin (16–20) ▼

164

Conus stercusmuscarum Linné (16–31) ▲

Conus ebraeus Linné (16–10) ▼

165
Conus aulicus Linné (16–21) ▲
Conus cedonulli Linné (16–13) ▼

165
Amoria undulata Lamarck (15–22) ▲
Conus striatus Linné (16–32) ▼

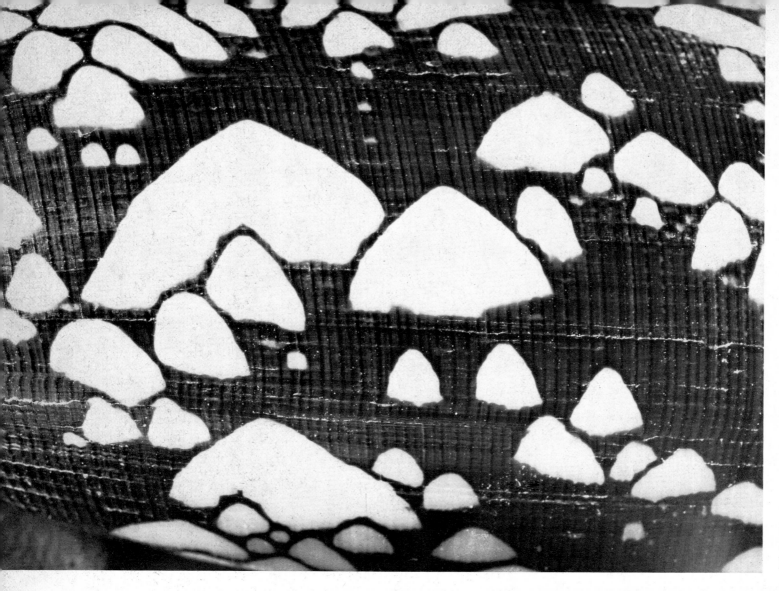

166
◀ *Conus aulicus* Linné
(16–21)

167
Lioconcha castrensis
Linné (30–3) ▶

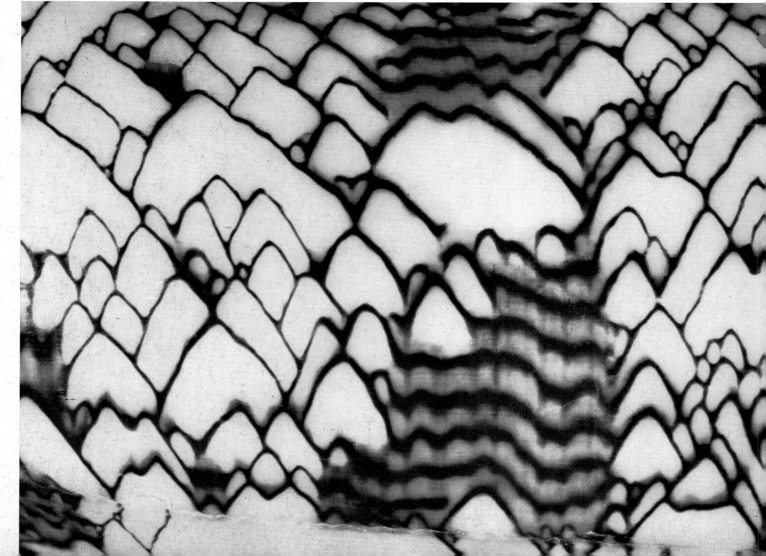

166
Conus textile Linné
(16–23) ▶

▲ 169 *Monodonta zebra* Menke (3–1)

◀ 168 *Strigatella paupercula* Linné (15–8); *Amoria macandrewi* Sowerby (15–23); *Tiara praestantissima* Röding (15–9)

▼ 169 *Clanculus pharaonius* Linné (3–8)

169 *Paralagena smaragdula* Linné (14–7) ▲

169 *Monodonta canalifera* Lamarck (3–2) ▼

170
▲ *Voluta musica* Linné (15–13) ▲

170
▼ *Conus marmoreus* Linné (16–8)

170
Conus figulinus Linné (16–27) ▼

171
Hydatina zonata Lightfoot (17–2) ▼

171
Volutoconus bednalli Brazier (15–17) ▲

172
◀ *Cerithium
fasciatum*
Bruguière
(6–7)

172
Amoria ellioti
Sowerby (15–21) ▶

172
Amoria zebra Leach
(15–24) ▶

173
Phasianella australis Linné (3–23)

174
▲ *Cypraea argus* Linné (10–4)

175
Cypraea mappa Linné (10–3) ▶

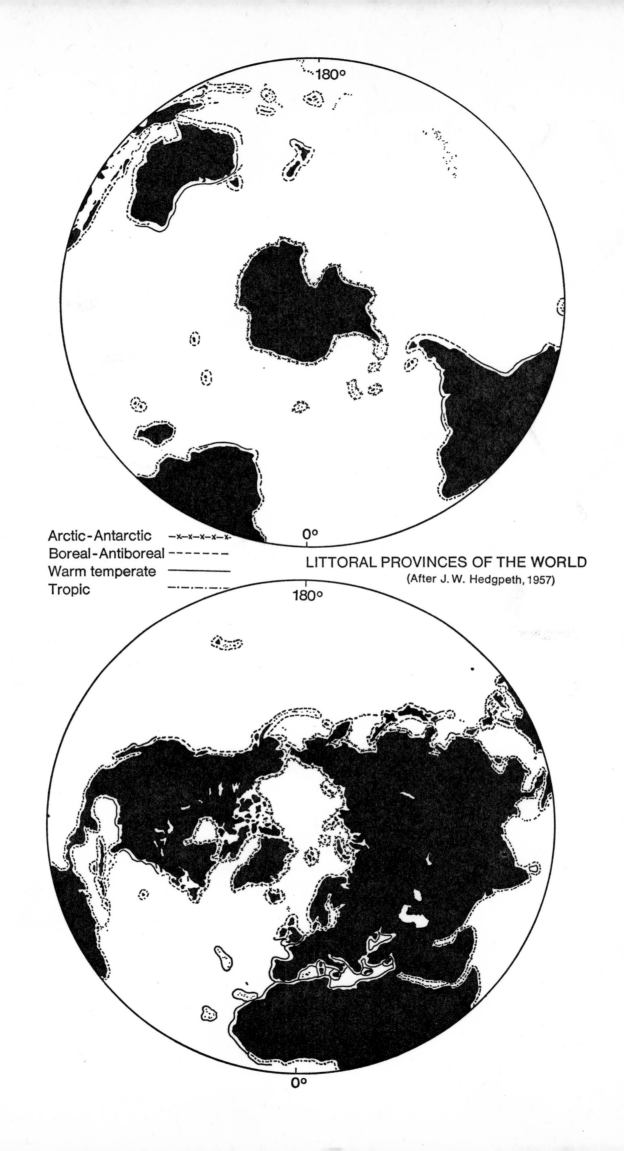

Arctic-Antarctic —x—x—x—x—x—
Boreal-Antiboreal - - - - - - - -
Warm temperate ————————
Tropic —·—·—·—·—

LITTORAL PROVINCES OF THE WORLD
(After J. W. Hedgpeth, 1957)

A Catalog of Marine Shells

This catalog brings together the names and pictures of what your photographer considers the world's most beautiful and interesting shells. They were chosen from one of the most comprehensive shell collections ever assembled, that of the American Museum of Natural History in New York.

In addition to providing guidance and inspiration for shell collectors and being a tribute to the almost infinite variety of form which shells can assume, the catalog also gives the reader an idea of the evolution and interrelationship of the various groups of marine shells, since, unlike the preceding part of the book, it presents the shells arranged in systematic order in accordance with the modern scheme of classification of the phylum Mollusca, the mollusks. Each species has been given a reference number consisting of the number of the superfamily to which it belongs combined with a number that indicates its place within the superfamily; this number will be found where each shell appears in the book, providing a cross reference from the pictures and text. Each shell is shown whole and in its actual size. The accompanying text was prepared and the whole project supervised by Dr. William K. Emerson, Curator of Mollusks and Chairman of the Department of Living Invertebrates of the American Museum of Natural History.

The purpose of scientific classification is two-fold: to assign each species its proper place in the natural order of living things in accordance with its evolutionary and morphological characteristics; and to enable scientists and interested laymen from all over the world to identify any known species and make sure that they all talk about the same animal or plant. This ambitious goal is accomplished by a complex but strictly logical system of groups within groups which in turn are subdivided into still smaller groups until a basic unit is reached, the species.

The *species* — a group of animals or plants of "the same kind" with virtually identical characteristics, although subject to some variation — is the basic building block in the system of scientific classification of living things. Species (the same form of the word serves as singular and plural) that have similar though not identical character-

istics, indicative of a close evolutionary relationship, are brought together in the next higher group, the *genus* (plural: *genera*). In turn, related genera are combined within a *family,* related families within a *superfamily,* and related superfamilies within an *order.* Related orders are brought together to form a *class,* and related classes constitute a *phylum* — in our case, the phylum Mollusca.

Within this all-encompassing scheme, order is established by arranging the different groups and subgroups in logical sequence in accordance with their evolutionary-morphological characteristics, placing those with the most primitive features at the beginning of the classification and those with the most highly evolved qualities at the end. In the case of the prosobranch snails, for instance, the slit shells and abalones represent some of the most primitive types of gastropods and the cones and terebras some of the most highly evolved.

Mollusks, like most other animals or plants, may be known by two names: popular and scientific. For example, abalone, scallop, oyster, and clam are popular names. More precisely, they are common names applied to broad groups of mollusks, each of which may contain many species. But even if amplified by qualifying terms like *Red* Abalone, *Noble* Scallop, *Pearl* Oyster, or *Razor* Clam, this kind of popular name has serious disadvantages that make it unsatisfactory for scientific purposes. Not only are popular names different in different languages and therefore not internationally understood, but their meaning is often unclear even to those who speak the same language because it often happens that a specific kind of shell goes under several different, regional names. The shell of the widely ranging gastropod genus *Haliotis,* for example, is known to English-speaking people as Abalone in California, Ormer in England, Ear Shell in Australia, Venus Ear Shell in South Africa, and Paua in New Zealand.

To avoid this confusion, scientists from all over the world have long since agreed to give each species of living thing a single latinized binomial name. This has important advantages. Latin is a "dead" language and therefore no longer subject to change. It is intelligible to scientific investigators from all countries, no matter what their native tongue. And it provides unambiguous identification even for those animals and plants (and there are thousands) that have no popular name.

The scientific name of every animal and plant consists of three words (occasionally four words in cases where subspecies are recognized). The Latin name of the Red Abalone, for example, is *Haliotis rufescens* Swainson. The first word, which is always capitalized, is the name of the genus (group of closely related species) to which the respective animal or plant belongs (analogous to a person's last or family name). The second word, which is usually descriptive, designates the particular species to which the specimen in question belongs (analogous to a person's first or given name). The names of the genus and species are always italicized. The third word (frequently given in abbreviated form) is the name of the author, the scientist who first described the respective species and published his findings in a scientific journal.

Being able to call a person by name immediately establishes a new relationship — less impersonal, friendlier, more enjoyable. The same is true of shells: a shell that you know by name becomes a friend that is recognized on sight and greeted with pleasure. Learning the names of mollusks — both popular and scientific — will greatly add to your enjoyment of shells.

— ANDREAS FEININGER

Class Gastropoda

The snails and their allies include mollusks with a distinct head, usually with eyes and tentacles, and with a foot adapted for crawling. The single shell, or univalve, is generally coiled. Gastropods, which number about 37,500 living species, live on land and in the sea and fresh water. Representatives of the major groups of marine gastropods are treated in this catalog.

Subclass Prosobranchia

Order Archaeogastropoda

1. Superfamily Pleurotomariacea

THE SLIT SHELLS
(Family Pleurotomariidae)

Slit shells are commonly represented in the fossil record, but only a dozen or so species of these colorful snails are known to be living. These occur in deep water in the Atlantic and western Pacific oceans. Specimens are rare in collections because they must be dredged or are encountered accidentally in fish traps. They are named for the long slit in the middle of the last whorl, which serves as an opening for the passage of water and waste products. One species is gigantic, reaching a diameter of 12 inches.

1-1 HIRASE'S SLIT SHELL, *Perotrochus hirasei* Pilsbry; off southern Japan; 3 to 5 inches in height, with a buff-colored base and reddish orange bands; commonest of the Slit Shells, often trawled by Japanese fishermen, in depths of 50 to 300 fathoms.

THE ABALONE SHELLS
(Family Haliotidae)

The abalone shell superficially resembles a large clam valve, with several holes that are used by the animal for the circulation of water and waste material. The top of the shell has a small spiral whorl; the inside is iridescent. The nearly one hundred species are world-wide in distribution and live on rocks, where they cling to the surface by a large muscular foot. Most species are found in shallow water, but a few occur in considerable depths. The foot is highly esteemed for food, and the iridescent shell is used in costume jewelry.

1-2 GREEN ABALONE, *Haliotis fulgens* Philippi; California to Baja California, Mexico; 7 to 8 inches in length; exterior dull reddish brown, interior iridescent blue and green; five or six open holes. (Pl. 106.)

Polished shells of RED ABALONE, *H. rufescens* Swainson (1-2a), and BLACK ABALONE, *H. cracherodii* Leach (1-2b), both west America, are shown in plates 119 and 120, respectively.

THE KEYHOLE LIMPETS
(Family Fissurellidae)

The keyhole limpets are a large family numbering more than five hundred living species. The shells are cap-shaped and resemble miniature volcanoes. They are usually conical, with an opening at the apex. As in the slit shells, the opening allows the passage of the exhalant currents. Most of the larger species live on rocks and boulders in the intertidal zone. Adults lack an operculum. The homing instinct is well developed in limpets. They crawl over the rocks to graze on seaweed, but they return to their original resting place.

1-3 DARWIN'S KEYHOLE LIMPET, *Fissurella darwini* Reeve; one of the smaller Chilean species; 1½ to 2 inches; shell dark outside, white interior, with a dark-colored border.

1-4 KNOBBY KEYHOLE LIMPET, *Fissurella nodosa* Born; Florida Keys and the West Indies; 1 to 1½ inches; solid white. Less common than other West Indian species.

2. Superfamily Patellacea

THE LIMPET SHELLS
(Family Patellidae)

The Old World limpets of the genus *Cellana* occur in the Indo-Pacific Province. The interior of the shell has a metallic, nacreous glaze, while in the shells of their relatives, the *Patella* limpets, the interior is porcellaneous.

2-1 BLACK-LINED LIMPET, *Cellana nigrolineata* Reeve; from Japan and the Ryukyus; 1½ to 3 inches; russet or blackish rayed outside, inside with an orange and white center. Often polished and made into brooches. (Pl. 39.)

2-2 HAWAIIAN LIMPET, *Cellana exarata* Nuttall; from Hawaiian Islands; 1 to 2½ inches; similar to the preceding but with raised black ribs on silvery shell. (Pl. 16.)

2-3 DARK-SCALED LIMPET, *Cellana nigrosquamata* Reeve; an uncommon species from Japan and the Bonin Islands; 2 to 4 inches; shell buff-colored, with raised, scalelike ribs.

2-4 WEAVED LIMPET, *Cellana denticulata* Martyn; from New Zealand; 2 inches; shell with brown ribs; resembles a woven basket.

2-5 ORNATE LIMPET, *Cellana ornata* Martyn; New Zealand; 1 to 2 inches; shell orange or silver with dark brown rays.

2-6 GOLDEN LIMPET, *Cellana radians flava* Hutton; 1 to 2 inches; a New Zealand race of *Cellana radians* that is golden orange.

THE CAP LIMPETS
(Family Acmaeidae)

These, the true limpets, are widely distributed but are most numerous on the west coast of North America. The homing instinct is well developed in acmaeids, which are vegetarians. About four hundred species are known. An operculum is lacking.

2-7 GREENISH CAP LIMPET, *Acmaea viridula* Lamarck; from Chile; 1 to 2½ inches; white with greenish rays. Uncommon. (Pl. 99.)

3. Superfamily Trochacea

THE TOP SHELLS (Family Trochidae)

These toplike shells are conical in shape and usually have a round aperture. Many have a beautiful nacreous interior. The operculum is usually thin, corneous, and circular in shape. These snails are vegetarians. The shells of many species have been used in the manufacture of buttons, mother-of-pearl ornaments, and jewelry. The animals of some of the larger species are used for food.

3-1 STRIPED MONODONT, *Monodonta zebra* Menke; from southeastern Australia; 1 inch; pale shell with black stripes. (Pl. 169.)

3-2 CHANNELED MONODONT, *Monodonta canalifera* Lamarck; Philippines to Ryukyus; 1 inch; greenish shell with spiral rows of dots and checks. (Pl. 169.)

3-3 BLACK GIBBULA, *Diloma sinensis* Gmelin; South Africa; 2 inches; solid black shell, brilliant pink columellar wall.

3-4 GREAT GIBBULA, *Gibbula magus* Linné; Mediterranean Sea; 1½ inches; brick red with pink markings.

3-5 QUEEN TEGULA, *Tegula regina* Stearns; off Southern California and western Mexico; 1½ to 2 inches; shell conic, purplish gray to black with a brilliant metallic golden stained columella and aperture. An uncommon species. (Pl. 105.)

3-6 VIRGATED TOP SHELL, *Trochus virgatus* Gmelin; Red Sea area; 2½ inches; white or pinkish with red-brown markings; base quite concave.

3-7 PYRAMID TOP SHELL, *Tectus pyramis* Born; Indo-Pacific Province generally; 5 inches; gray-green in color; shell usually heavily eroded. Long used in ornament manufacture. (Pl. 109.)

3-8 BLACK-LINED STRAWBERRY SHELL, *Clanculus pharaonius* Linné; Red Sea; 1 inch; red with alternating bands of black. A popular collector's item. (Pl. 169.)

THE DOLPHIN SHELLS
(Family Angariidae)

These flat-topped shells have a large aperture with the whorls keeled and spinose. These snails live on or near coral reefs.

3-9 TARANTULA DOLPHIN SHELL, *Angaria melanacantha* Reeve; southern Philippines; 3 inches; a rather rare shell, with projecting recurved spines. (Pl. 8.)

THE TURBAN AND STAR SHELLS
(Family Turbinidae)

A large family of globular shells with a rounded aperture and body whorl. The common name is derived from a fanciful resemblance to a turban. The operculum is shelly or porcellaneous and is often referred to as a cat's eye. In the star shells (*Astraea* and relatives), the juvenile shell is usually flattened but develops a pyramidal form as whorls are added. The aperture is usually elliptical in shape. These shells are vegetarians, feeding on marine algae.

3-10 WAVY TOP SHELL, *Astraea undosa* Wood; California to Baja California, Mexico; 2 to 6 inches in height; shell brown with raised wavy ribs.

3-11 GREENISH TOP SHELL, *Astraea olivacea* Wood; west Mexico; 3 inches; shell greenish to green, maculated with brown; base paler, with a brick red columellar area.

3-12 SUPERB STAR SHELL, *Astraea stellare* Gmelin; northwest Australia; 2 to 2½ inches; cream with a cerulean blue operculum and columellar wall. The color blue is extremely rare in molluscan shells; this is one of the few species that have blue pigment in their shells.

3-13 HELIOTROPE STAR SHELL, *Astraea heliotropium* Martyn; trawled in deep water, New Zealand; 3 to 5 inches; shell silvery nacreous overlaid with an outer layer of purplish brown, aperture nacreous, operculum white. Formerly considered a choice collector's item, but no longer a rarity. (Pl. 17.)

3-14 YELLOW STAR SHELL, *Astralium calcar* Linné; Philippines and adjacent areas; 2 to 2½ inches; shell cream with pronounced spines, throat of aperture greenish yellow. A colorful and popular shell. (Pl. 135.)

3-15 TRIUMPHANT STAR SHELL, *Guildfordia triumphans* Philippi; in deep water off Japan and adjacent areas of the Western Pacific; 2½ to 3½ inches; metallic purplish above and paler white below; seven to nine spines radiate from the body whorl, spines somewhat truncated and shorter than those of the next species. A very popular shell. (Pl. 22.)

3-16 IMPERIAL STAR SHELL, *Guildfordia yoka* Jousseaume; deep water off Japan; 1 to 5 inches in diameter; spines are long and well developed. Shell is rather rare. (Pl. 14.)

3-17 GLORIOUS STAR SHELL, *Guildfordia henicus gloriosa* Kuroda; deep water off Japan; 1 inch; rare cream-colored species.

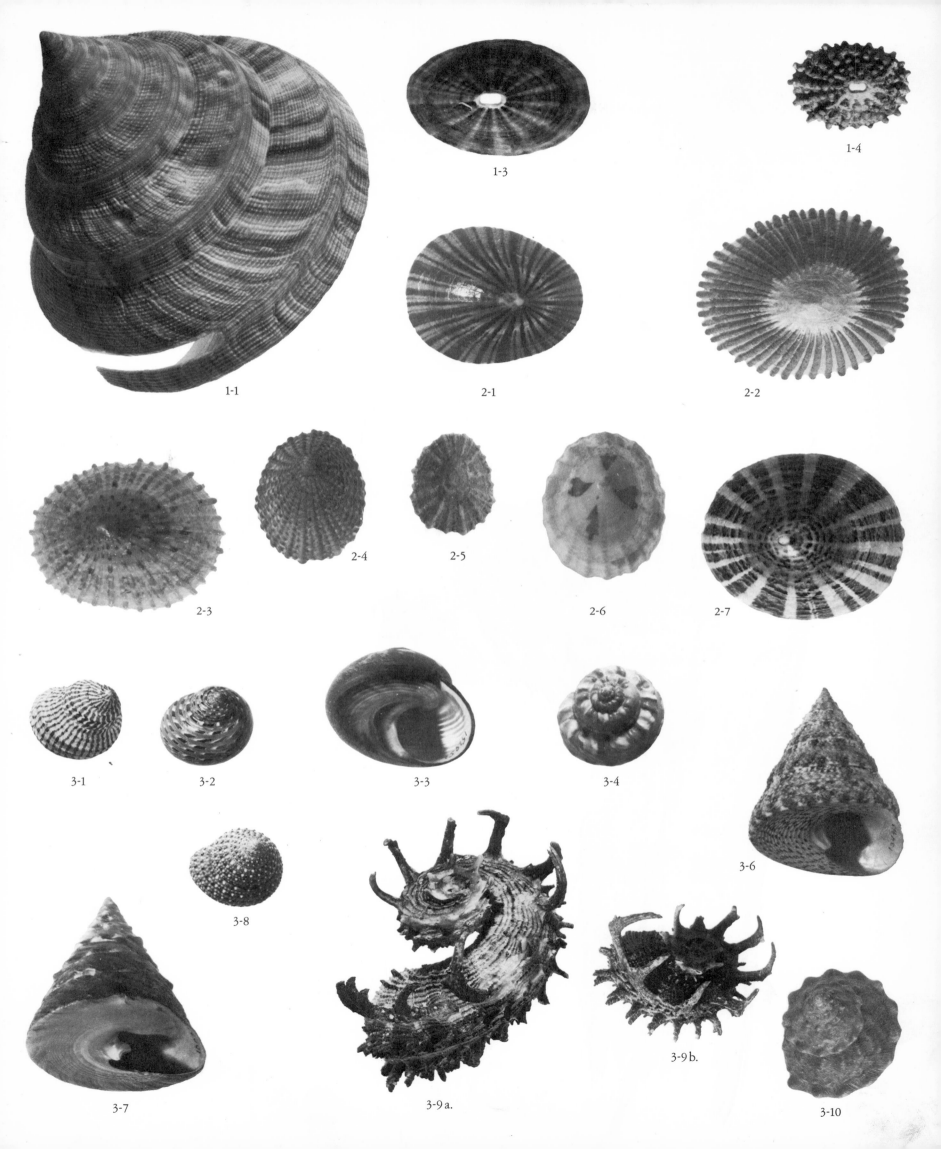

1-1

1-3

1-4

2-1

2-2

2-3

2-4

2-5

2-6

2-7

3-1

3-2

3-3

3-4

3-6

3-8

3-7

3-9 a.

3-9 b.

3-10

3-18 REEVE'S TURBAN SHELL, *Turbo reevei* Philippi; Philippines and Western Pacific; 2 to 3 inches; very similar to the Cat's Eye Turban (*Turbo petholatus* Linné); shell thinner; columella and operculum usually white; shell variegated brown, green, or orange. (Pl. 117.)

3-19 GOLD-MOUTH TURBAN, *Turbo chrysostomus* Linné; Indo-Pacific; 2 to 3 inches. An attractive and widely distributed species; long used in the novelty trade. (Pl. 113.)

3-20 GREEN-LINED TURBAN, *Turbo speciosus* Reeve; Queensland, Australia; 2 to 3 inches; similar to the preceding and to the Silver-lipped Turban, but ribs jade green. (Pl. 116.)

3-21 VARIABLE TURBAN, *Turbo fluctuosus* Wood; from Mexico to Peru; 3 inches; shell variable, commonly brownish, operculum green and white with raised spiral ribs. (Pl. 79.)

3-22 TURK'S CAP, *Turbo sarmaticus* Linné; South Africa; 3 to 5 inches; outer layer thin and often eroded, revealing pearly nacreous layer below; operculum with raised pustules. Both operculum and shell have been used as jewelry or novelties for centuries. (Pls. 9, 78.)

3-22a GREEN TURBAN SNAIL, *Turbo marmoratus* Linné; Indo-Pacific; 5 to 9 inches; largest species of the genus. Greenish outer layer may be removed, revealing the iridescent nacreous layer. Has been used as an ornament and in the manufacture of buttons, etc. The large white operculum (shown in pl. 84) is often used as a paperweight.

THE PHEASANT SHELLS
(Family Phasianellidae)

These shells derive their name from the beautiful variegated coloration which is reminiscent of the plumage of pheasants. The surface is glazed, with a chalky layer underneath. The operculum is shelly. The approximately forty species are widely distributed in tropical and temperate waters of the world; most species have thin shells. The living pheasant snails are capable of autotomy; that is, a portion of the foot is detached if it is seized by an enemy. Pheasant shells deteriorate if kept in damp surroundings.

3-23 AUSTRALIAN PHEASANT SHELL, *Phasianella australis* Linné; largest species of the family, 2½ to 3½ inches in height; one of the most variable of all shells in pattern and coloration. Uncommon. (Pl. 173.)

4. Superfamily Neritacea

THE NERITE SHELLS
(Family Neritidae)

Nerite shells have habits similar to periwinkles. They are usually found on rocks at or above the high-water line. While periwinkles are characteristic of northern shores, nerites are found throughout the tropical and temperate zones, not only along shores but also in estuaries, and many species of *Neritina* are found far up rivers in fresh water. The operculum is shelly. All are vegetarians.

4-1 TEXTILE NERITE, *Nerita textilis* Gmelin; Indo-Pacific Province, but perhaps best known from the East Africa coastline and Indian Ocean islands; 1½ to 2 inches in length, one of the larger species of the family. (Pl. 141.)

Order Mesogastropoda

5. Superfamily Littorinacea

THE PERIWINKLES (Family Littorinidae)

The periwinkles are a rather large family; some two hundred species have been described. They are one of the characteristic forms of life on rocky shores in the northern hemisphere. However, there are many species that inhabit littoral tropical waters. They are found on tree trunks, grasses, pilings, and other substrates near the shore. The operculum is horny. Some species lay eggs in capsules, while in others the eggs are hatched internally. These vegetarians are able to survive for long periods out of water and some species can tolerate a wide range of salinities.

5-1 NORTHERN PERIWINKLE, *Littorina littorea* Linné; reputedly introduced to the New World from Europe; ¾ inch is the normal size, though an occasional specimen may reach 2 inches in height. Perhaps one of the best known sea snails; commonly eaten in parts of England and Europe; a common species along the northeastern coast of North America.

5-2 PAGODA WINKLE, *Tectarius pagodus* Linné; Philippines, Melanesia, and other areas of the Western Pacific; about 3½ inches in height, this is considered the giant of the family.

5-3 PRICKLY WINKLE, *Tectarius tectumpersicum* Linné; from the Indo-Pacific generally; at 1 inch, a smaller edition of the above; more knobby in general appearance.

6. Superfamily Cerithiacea

THE TURRET SHELLS
(Family Turritellidae)

These herbivorous snails have long, thin shells with many whorls and encircling ridges. They may be easily distinguished from auger shells (*Terebridae*, 16-35–16-39) by their rounded apertures; the apertures of auger shells are elliptical in shape. About fifty species are known from temperate to tropical waters; several hundred fossil species have been described. The round operculum is horny.

3-11

3-12

3-13

3-14

3-15

3-16

3-17

3-18

3-19

3-20

3-21

3-22

3-23

3-23

4-1

5-1

5-2

5-3

6-1 GREAT SCREW SHELL, *Turritella terebra* Linné; Indian Ocean and Western Pacific; attains a length of 3 to 5 inches; brown or purplish brown. Its elegant shape and fine spiral sculpture make it one of the handsomest species in the family. (Pls. 28, 58, 140.)

A related species, the BANDED SCREW SHELL, *T. duplicata* Linné (6-1a), from the Indian Ocean, is shown in plate 141.

THE SUNDIAL SHELLS
(Family Architectonicidae)

The sundial shells, instead of being tapered like the preceding, are widely coiled and recall a flattened, winding staircase. Most are brown or tan with spiral lines of dark brown and white. The base of the shell is remarkable: it is widely opened and umbilicated, with a beaded, spiral ridge resembling a circular staircase. The operculum is horny. All forty living species are tropical.

6-2 ORIENTAL SUNDIAL, *Architectonica perspectivum* Linné; tropical Indo-Pacific; at 2½ inches it is characteristic of the family; related species from Japan attain a larger size, but all are superficially similar. (Pl. 93.)

THE WORM SHELLS (Family Vermetidae)

These snails receive their vernacular name from their resemblance to worm tubes. While many kinds of marine worms do secrete or construct shells or tubes, the worm shells begin life as typical gastropod snails. In early life they resemble turret shells; later they begin to grow erratically. They live in clusters or embedded in sponges. The thin operculum is horny.

6-3 WEST INDIAN WORM SHELL, *Vermicularia spirata* Philippi; inhabits southeastern Florida and the West Indies; 3 inches or larger; horn-brown in color. A common species. (Pl. 32.)

THE TELESCOPE SHELLS
(Family Potamididae)

These are a tropical family. Also called "creepers," they are inhabitants of estuarial mud flats. Their shells are often badly eroded because of the highly nitrogenous content of the brackish water. The horny operculum is circular.

6-4 QUEENSLAND CREEPER, *Pyrazus eberninus* Bruguière; common in parts of Queensland, Australia, and elsewhere; 3 to 5 inches; a rather strikingly shaped shell, dark brown with a widely flaring lip. (Pl. 36.)

6-5 DUSKY CREEPER, *Tympanotomus fuscatus* Linné; inhabitant of swamps and estuarine bays along the west coast of Africa; at 2 inches, it is somewhat smaller than the preceding in size; shell is often heavily eroded. (Pl. 36.)

6-6 HUMBOLDT'S CREEPER, *Rhinocoryne humboldti* Valenciennes; from the west coast of Central America southward to Chile; 1½ inches; similar to *Pyrazus* but smaller and attractively marked in slate blue with a white aperture. (Pl. 57.)

THE HORN SHELLS (Family Cerithiidae)

The horn shells, a rather large family of snails, are distributed in shallow water throughout the tropical and subtropical belts of the world. There are about three hundred living species and also many fossil species, some of which attained gigantic proportions. The horny operculum has a few whorls.

6-7 BANDED HORN SNAIL, *Cerithium fasciatum* Bruguière; Indo-Pacific region; 2½ to 3 inches; shell white or ivory with brown bands; perhaps the prettiest of the genus. (Pl. 172.)

6-8 GIANT CREEPER, *Campanile symbolicum* Tate; Western Australia; attains a size of 6 inches or more and is the largest living species of the horn shell family; shell white, though often heavily eroded; aperture small, thin, and lacking a flaring lip, giving an immature appearance. Not common in collections. (Pl. 37.)

7. Superfamily Epitoniacea

THE WENTLETRAPS (Family Epitoniidae)

These are strikingly beautiful little shells and highly esteemed by shell collectors. Those who profess not to like small shells usually make an exception in this case. The vernacular name, wentletrap, is believed to have been derived from the German word *Wendeltreppe,* a spiral staircase. Usually glazed white in color, these shells are ornamented with evenly spaced, raised axial ribs. The horny operculum is round or semi-crescentic. Nearly three hundred species are known, many of which inhabit deep water. They feed on sea anemones and other invertebrates and exude a purple dye which may serve as an anesthetic.

7-1 PRECIOUS WENTLETRAP, *Epitonium scalare* Linné; from a wide range in the Western Pacific Ocean; 2½ to 3 inches in height. (Pls. 86, 95.)

7-2 MAGNIFICENT WENTLETRAP, *Amaea magnifica* Sowerby; up to 5 inches in length; perhaps the largest of the living species of wentletrap, it is an uncommon Japanese species. The surface is covered with a fretwork of fine, raised ribs. (Pls. 37, 134.)

THE VIOLET SNAILS
(Family Janthinidae)

These are pelagic species that are often washed

6-2

6-3

6-4

6-5

6-6

6-1

6-7

6-8

7-1

7-2

7-3

8-1

8-2

8-3

9-1

9-2

ashore in great numbers. They secrete a raft of bubbles and float with colonies of hydroids, upon which they feed. Violet snails lack eyes. An operculum occurs only in the larval stage.

7-3 VIOLET SNAIL, *Janthina janthina* Linné; 2 to 2½ inches; violet below and white above, which is reversed in life, as they float in an inverted position beneath their "bubble raft"; pelagic in warm water in all seas. (Pl. 120.)

8. Superfamily Calyptraeacea

THE SLIPPER AND CUP-AND-SAUCER SHELLS (Family Calyptraeidae)

These limpetlike shells have a plate that resembles a cup or a shelf inside the main shell; they adhere to stones or other shells in shallow water.

8-1 EXTENDED SLIPPER SHELL, *Crepidula dilatata* Lamarck; Peru and Chile; 2½ inches; a large flat, white species, with the septum unattached at the right edge.

8-2 ONYX SLIPPER SHELL, *Crepidula onyx* Sowerby; Southern California to Chile; 1½ inches; attractive species, chocolate brown with a white septum.

8-3 STRIATE CUP-AND-SAUCER, *Crucibulum striatum* Say; east coast of North America; 1 to 1½ inches; orange-brown with white central cup. Sometimes trawled attached to shells or stones; rarely found intertidally.

9. Superfamily Strombacea

THE CARRIER SHELLS (Family Xenophoridae)

These snails have been frequently referred to as "the original shell-collectors" because of their habit of cementing other shells, bits of coral, or stones to their own shell. Fewer than fifty living species are known. The species found in deep water are poorer collectors than those from shallow depths. The thin, horny operculum is fan-shaped.

9-1 SUNBURST CARRIER, *Xenophora solaris* Linné; deep water in the Western Pacific; 3 to 5 inches; unique among carriers in the possession of long spines, somewhat like those of *Guildfordia* (3-15).

9-2 LONGLEY'S CARRIER, *Tugurium longleyi* Bartsch; largest and rarest of the three species of carriers inhabiting the western Atlantic; 5 to 9 inches. This deep-water species often has rare or unusual shells attached. (Pl. 50.)

9-3 PALLID CARRIER, *Xenophora pallidula* Reeve; Indo-Pacific generally, most widely ranging species of the family; 3 to 5 inches; similar to the Atlantic Carrier, *X. conchyliophora*, but base paler in color. (Pls. 48, 51, 54, 55.)

9-4 MEXICAN CARRIER, *Xenophora robusta* Verrill; west Mexico; 3 to 5 inches in diameter; similar to *X. conchyliophora* but much greater in height. (Pl. 53.)

9-5 PERON'S CARRIER, *Xenophora peronianus* Iredale; an uncommon species from the east coast of Australia; 3 inches. (Pl. 54.)

9-6 WRINKLED CARRIER, *Xenophora corrugata* Reeve; Western Pacific; 3 inches; less common than *X. pallidula* from same region; base with ripples instead of smooth. (Pls. 49, 52, 53.)

THE PELICAN'S FOOT SHELLS (Family Aporrhaidae)

These shells have an expanded, flaring lip resembling a bird's foot. The narrow operculum is horny. Less than a dozen species have been described, all from the North Atlantic and the Mediterranean.

9-7 WEST AFRICAN PELICAN'S FOOT, *Aporrhais serresianus* Michaud; West Africa; 2 inches; uncommon species with long, pointed digitations.

9-8 AMERICAN PELICAN'S FOOT, *Aporrhais occidentalis* Beck; North Atlantic; 2 to 3 inches; olivaceous deep-water shell. Occasionally trawled by fishermen.

THE CONCH SHELLS (Family Strombidae)

Tibias, conchs, and scorpion shells all belong to the family Strombidae. While many shells are called conchs in the vernacular, it is to shells of this family that the name properly belongs. Conchs occur in all warm-water oceans with the exception of the Mediterranean Sea. Tibias and scorpion shells are found in the Indo-Pacific Province. The horny operculum is sickle-shaped. About eighty living species form the family.

9-9 SPINDLE TIBIA or RAT-TAIL TIBIA, *Tibia fusus* Linné; Western Pacific; 6 to 10 inches; a rich brown colored shell trawled from depths of 70 to 100 fathoms or more. Very popular with collectors. (Pls. 30, 74.)

9-10 MARTINI'S TIBIA, *Tibia martinii* Marrat; Western Pacific; 5 to 6 inches; rather fragile; occasionally dredged from depths of about 150 fathoms. Uncommon in collections. (Pl. 30.)

9-11 PINK CONCH or QUEEN CONCH, *Strombus gigas* Linné; Florida Keys and West Indies; 8 to 12 inches. With its brilliant rose aperture, this is one of the best known shells. Legislation now offers some protection in Florida. The flesh is a staple item of diet in parts of the Caribbean area. Occasionally produces pretty, pink pearls. (Pl. 104.)

9-12 ROOSTER CONCH, *Strombus gallus* Linné; Caribbean; 4 to 5 inches; a choice species with

9-3

9-5

9-4

9-6

9-7

9-9

9-8

9-10

9-12

9-9

9-13

9-14

9-15

9-16

9-11

9-17

9-18

9-19

9-20

9-21

9-22

9-23

9-24

10-1

10-2

10-3

10-6

10-4

10-4

10-5

10-7

a produced "wing." Popular collector's item. (Pl. 18.)

9-13 LAVENDER CONCH, *Strombus sinuatus* Lightfoot; Western Pacific; 4 to 5 inches; a beautiful species with digitated lip and violet aperture. (Pl. 20.)

9-14 DIANA'S EAR, *Strombus aurisdianae* Linné; Indo-Pacific; 2 to 3 inches. A common and widely distributed species, one of the commonest of the Pacific shells. (Pl. 20.)

9-15 IREDALE'S CONCH, *Strombus vomer iredalei* Abbott; northwest Australia; 2 to 3 inches; similar to the preceding. Uncommon. (Pls. 21, 141.)

9-16 DOVE CONCH, *Strombus plicatus columba* Lamarck; Indian Ocean islands and East Africa; 2 inches; attractive ivory-colored shell. (Pl. 21.)

9-17 CHIRAGRA SPIDER, *Lambis chiragra* Linné; Western Pacific; 5 to 9 inches, large and striking member of the scorpion shell genus; pink aperture. A popular and well known species. (Pl. 126.)

9-18 ARTHRITIC SPIDER, *Lambis chiragra arthritica* Röding; a race of the preceding species restricted to the Indian Ocean; 3 to 5 inches; similar to the preceding but with an aperture with numerous wrinkles and purplish brown in coloration. (Pls. 29, 75.)

9-19 SPIDER CONCH, *Lambis lambis* Linné; Indo-Pacific; 4 to 8 inches; a well known species with a pinkish orange aperture. Males mature at a smaller size than females. (Pl. 148.)

9-20 PILSBRY'S SPIDER, *Lambis crocata pilsbryi* Abbott; uncommon race endemic to Marquesas; 8 to 10 inches. (Pl. 19.)

9-21 MILLEPEDE SPIDER, *Lambis millepeda* Linné; southwestern Pacific; 4 to 5 inches; brown with purplish brown aperture. Common species. (Pl. 149.)

9-22 VIOLET SPIDER, *Lambis violacea* Swainson; Mauritius; 3 to 4 inches; white with violet aperture. A rare collector's item. (Pls. 18, 156.)

9-23 ELONGATE SPIDER, *Lambis digitata* Perry; Indo-Pacific; 3 to 5 inches; tan with lemon yellow aperture. A wide-ranging, yet uncommon species. (Pls. 20, 76.)

9-24 SCORPION SHELL, *Lambis scorpius* Linné; Western Pacific; orange with purple aperture. Fairly common. (Pl. 23.)

10. Superfamily Cypraeacea

THE COWRIES (Family Cypraeidae)

Cowries, with their rich, polished shells and intricate patterns, have been used by man as ornaments for millenia, long before the advent of shell collecting. There are more than two hundred living species of cowries, occurring in all tropical and warm seas. They lack an operculum. They live from the littoral zone down to depths of more than 100 fathoms. Sexual dimorphism is common; the shell of the male is usually smaller. The early growth stage of the shell is thin-lipped and resembles an immature olive shell.

10-1 HOWELL'S COWRIE, *Cypraea hesitata howelli* Iredale; trawled off southeast Australia; 3 to 4 inches; deep-water form of the Wonder Cowrie, *C. hesitata.* Formerly rather rare, today available in limited quantities. (Pl. 111.)

10-2 GOLDEN COWRIE, *Cypraea aurantium* Gmelin; southwest Pacific; 3½ to 5 inches. Most popular shell today; reputed to have been Fijian chieftain's property in the past, today it has become a status symbol among collectors; uncommon. (Pl. 111.)

10-3 MAP COWRIE, *Cypraea mappa* Linné; Indo-Pacific generally; 2¼ to 3¼ inches; brown pattern on the dorsum having an outline resembling a map. Another popular species. (Pl. 175.)

10-4 EYED COWRIE, *Cypraea argus* Linné; Indo-Pacific; 2½ to 4 inches; olivaceous shell with ocellations resembling eye spots. Also very popular. (Pl. 174.)

10-5 EGG COWRIE, *Ovula ovum* Linné; Indo-Pacific; 2½ to 4 inches. Very common intertidal species; allied to the cowries but placed in a different subfamily; sometimes mistaken for Howell's Cowrie by novices. (Pl. 35.)

10-6 SHUTTLECOCK or SPINDLE EGG SHELL, *Volva volva* Linné; Western Pacific; 3 to 5 inches; pinkish with a flaring lip and produced extremities. Popular with collectors. (Pl. 25).

10-7 LAVENDER SPINDLE, *Volva birostris* Linné; Western Pacific; 1 to 1½ inches; a delicate, elongate shell, lavender with a cream-colored margin. Lives on soft coral. Uncommon. (Pl. 31.)

11. Superfamily Naticacea

THE MOON SNAILS (Family Naticidae)

Moon snails are a large family of carnivorous sand dwellers. They wander along the bottom seeking clams or other prey, whose flesh they devour after drilling a neat, saucer-shaped hole in the shell. The true Naticas have a shelly operculum, whereas *Polinices* and its close relatives have a horny or corneous operculum.

11-1 ZEBRA MOON SNAIL, *Natica zebra* Lamarck; Western Pacific; 1 inch; a handsome shell, cream with brown axial lines.

11-2 VARIABLE MOON SNAIL, *Natica variolaria* Recluz; Indo-Pacific; 1½ inches; another attractive species, orange markings on cream with a lavender columella.

11-3 GLEAMING MOON SNAIL, *Polinices glauca* Humboldt; Peru and Chile; 2 to 3 inches; a tan shell of a depressed, globular shape. Uncommon.

11-4 SOUTHERN MOON SNAIL, *Polinices duplicatus* Say; east coast of the United States, Massachusetts to Texas; 2 to 3 inches; purplish brown. A common sand dweller, often found along our east-coast beaches. Florida specimens are larger and paler in coloration. (Pls. 84, 94.)

11-5 NORTHERN MOON SNAIL, *Lunatia heros* Say; Canada southward to North Carolina; 2 to 5 inches. Ivory to gray in color, with a more globular shell than the preceding species. Open umbilicus, lacking a callus. (A sectioned shell is shown in plate 58.)

12. Superfamily Tonnacea

THE HELMET SHELLS (Family Cassidae)

Helmets are another well known family of shells. Though used as ornaments for centuries, more recently they have been made into cameos and other jewelry, the varicolored layers of the shell producing a cameo of two or more colors. The operculum, when present, is horny. Most species inhabit rather shallow waters where they feed on echinoderms. About seventy living species are known. The shell of the female is generally larger than that of the male.

12-1 HORNED HELMET, *Cassis cornuta* Linné; Indo-Pacific; 8 to 12 inches; a large shell with a thickened, glazed lip. (Pls. 69, 86.)

12-2 AREOLE HELMET, *Phalium areola* Linné; Indo-Pacific; 3 to 3½ inches; slate gray, attractively marked with squarish brown checks. Fairly uncommon

12-3 CROSSED HELMET, *Phalium decussatum* Linné; Formosa and Western Pacific; 3 inches; similar to the Areole Helmet but the surface of the shell is finely sculptured rather than smooth.

12-4 FLAMED HELMET, *Phalium decussatum* var. *flammeolum* Röding; Formosa; 3 inches; a color form of the preceding in which the spots have coalesced into stripes or "flames."

12-5 SCOTCH BONNET, *Phalium granulatum* Born; North Carolina to Gulf of Mexico and West Indies; 2 to 3 inches; a cream-colored shell. (Pl. 137.)

12-6 WHITE GALEODES, *Galeodes leucodoma* Dall; a rather rare deep-water species trawled off Japan; 3 to 3½ inches; similar to the above but pure white, with a more sculptured shell. (Pl. 137.)

THE TRITON SHELLS
(Family Cymatiidae)

Triton shells are a family of more than one hundred living species. They range in size from the large trumpet shells of up to 20 inches in length, to a number of small, inch-long species. Many species possess a hairy outer covering of the shell. They are carnivorous.

12-7 WASHER TRITON, *Cymatium lotorium* Linné; Indo-Pacific; 3½ to 5 inches; attractive orange-brown shell with dark markings on the lip; lives on coral reefs.

12-8 GEM TRITON, *Cymatium rubeculum* Linné; Indo-Pacific; 1 to 2 inches; small, attractive shell, occurs in several color forms. (Pls. 21, 140.)

12-9 WRITHED DISTORTED SHELL, *Distorsio perdistorta* Fulton; off Japan; 2 to 2½ inches; a typical member of a group of about eleven species; the distorted shells are found in tropical and warm waters. (Pl. 72.)

THE TUN SHELLS (Family Tonnidae)

The tun shells belong to a small family of large, inflated, and rather thin shells. Typical tun shells have a thin lip and widely flaring aperture. An operculum is lacking in adults. These carnivorous snails engulf their prey, which are partially digested in the oral cavity by the aid of acid saliva.

12-10 GRINNING TUN, *Malea ringens* Swainson; west Mexico to Peru; 4 to 8 inches; one of the few species with a thickened, reflected lip. The labial denticles give the impression of a jack-o'-lantern or a grinning mouth, hence the vernacular name. (Pls. 6, 77.)

12-10a BLACK-LINED TUN SHELL, *Tonna melanostoma* Jay; Western Pacific; 4 to 10 inches; shell cream to mottled tan, aperture and columella stained a deep chestnut; alternating large and small ribs on the body whorl, grooves of small ribs chestnut to black stained. An uncommon species, seldom seen in collections. (Pls. 71, 83, 137.)

A more common spotted species, the SPOTTED TUN SHELL, *T. luteostoma* Küster (12-10b), from Japan, is shown in plate 96.

THE FIG SHELLS (Family Ficidae)

This group of sand-dwelling carnivorous snails is represented by about a dozen living species in the tropical seas. The large, fleshy foot is larger than the thin shell. An operculum is lacking.

12-11 DUSSUMIER'S FIG SHELL, *Ficus dussumieri* Valenciennes; Western Pacific; 3 to 6 inches; an elegant shell, brown with a dark purplish brown aperture. (Pl. 129.)

12-12 FILE FIG SHELL, *Ficus filosus* Sowerby; deep water off Japan; tan with cancellate sculpture, spiral ridges brown. Rare. (Pl. 15.)

13-11

13-12

13-13

13-14

13-15

13-16

13-17

13-18

13-19

13-20

13-21

13-22

13-23

13-24

13-25

13-26

13-27

13-28

13-29

13-30

13-31

13-32

13-33

13-34

13-35

Order Neogastropoda

13. Superfamily Muricacea

THE MUREX OR ROCK SHELLS
(Family Muricidae)

The Murex family is a very large one, containing many genera and several hundred species. They occur in nearly all waters except near the poles. Some of the most oddly shaped and spectacular of all shells are found in this family. The operculum is horny. These carnivorous snails prey on bivalves and other mollusks or eat freshly killed marine animals.

13-1 PAGODA SHELL, *Columbarium pagoda* Lesson; Japan and Western Pacific; 2½ to 3 inches; small, dark brown shell of unusual form; canal long, body with projecting spines. Uncommon.

13-2 VENUS COMB, *Murex triremis* Perry; Japan and Western Pacific; 4 to 6 inches; one of the most spectacular of shells, recalls a fish skeleton in form. (Pls. 1, 145.)

13-3 TROSCHEL'S MUREX, *Murex troscheli* Lischke; fairly deep water off Japan; 5 to 8 inches; an elegant shell, cream with brown lines. (Pl. 58.)

13-4 DARK-SPINED MUREX, *Murex tribulus nigrospinosus* Reeve; Philippines and adjacent areas; 4 to 5 inches; similar to the true Venus Comb shell, with tip of spines often blackish.

13-5 TERNISPINE MUREX, *Murex ternispina* Lamarck; Indo-Pacific; 4 inches; fewer and slightly shorter spines than the preceding species. (Pl. 30.)

13-6 RECURVED MUREX, *Murex recurvirostris* Broderip; west Mexico south to Ecuador; 2 inches; similar to preceding but smaller; dirty white or banded with brown.

13-7 HIRASE'S MUREX, *Murex hirasei* Hirase; off Japan and Western Pacific; 2½ inches. Named by Hirase the Elder for his son. A choice species, rare.

13-8 LONG-TAILED SNIPEBILL, *Haustellum longicaudum* Baker; Indo-Pacific; 3 to 5½ inches. It has been expounded that the long spines of the Comb Murex serve to protect them from predatory fish; yet this species, which inhabits the same waters as the species with long "protective" spines, is practically denuded.

13-9 HORNED MUREX, *Murex cornutus* Linné; West Africa; 4 to 7 inches; a large and unusual shell with two rows of heavy, reflected spines. Not common. (Pls. 144, 157.)

13-10 DYE MUREX, *Murex brandaris* Linné; Mediterranean Sea; 3 to 5 inches; a smaller species but otherwise quite similar to the preceding Horned Murex. One of the species used by the ancient Phoenicians, and later by the Greeks and Romans, in the preparation of dye, Tyrian purple.

13-11 DEER ANTLER MUREX, *Murex cervicornis* Lamarck; northwest Australia; 2½ to 3 inches; a superb species with bifurcated spines; lives in crevices in coral. Uncommon. (Pls. 30, 147.)

13-12 GREAT STAG-ANTLER MUREX, *Hexaplex cornucervi* Röding; northwest Australia; 3½ to 5 inches; another fine species with long, recurved spines; better known as *Murex monodon* Sowerby, a later name. (Pl. 155.)

13-13 ENDIVE or CHICORY MUREX, *Hexaplex cichoreus* Gmelin; Indo-Pacific; 3 to 4 inches; quite variable in coloration, from nearly black to pure white. A very common species that has long been used in the commercial shell trade. (Pls. 5, 118, 154.)

13-14 JAPANESE MUREX, *Chicoreus asianus* Kuroda; Japan; 3 to 4 inches; brown shell. Not uncommon. (Pl. 4.)

13-14a BRANCHED MUREX, *Chicoreus ramosus* Linné; Indo-Pacific; 4 to 12 inches. Largest species of the family. Shell white to brown, aperture rose pink. Varices with recurved spines. (Pl. 70; entire shell not shown.)

13-15 ROSE-BRANCH MUREX, *Chicoreus palmarosae* Lamarck; Ceylon and Western Pacific; 3 to 4½ inches; a beautiful shell with magenta-colored spines. Very popular with collectors. (Pls. 34, 151.)

13-16 LITTLE-LEAF MUREX, *Chicoreus microphyllus* Linné; Indo-Pacific; 2 to 3 inches; an attractive shell, cream with darker markings. Uncommon.

13-17 WEST INDIAN MUREX, *Chicoreus brevifrons* Lamarck; Florida Keys and West Indies; 3 to 5 inches; coloration variable. A common Caribbean species. (Pl. 158.)

13-18 LACE MUREX, *Chicoreus dilectus* A. Adams; west coast of Florida; 2½ inches; a well known white shell with leafy spines. Better known as *Murex arenarius* Clench, a later name. (Pl. 156.)

13-19 ACULEATE MUREX, *Chicoreus aculeatus* Lamarck; Western Pacific; 1½ to 2 inches; an attractive orange shell. Not common.

13-20 BURNT MUREX, *Chicoreus brunneus* Link; Indo-Pacific; 2½ to 3½ inches; usually dark brown or black with a pink aperture. A very common species; better known under the name *Murex adustus* Lamarck, a later name. (Pl. 19.)

13-21 BANK'S MUREX, *Chicoreus* c/f *banksi* Sowerby; northern Australia; 2½ inches; an uncommon brown shell. Often labeled "*axicornis,*" which is a smaller and different species.

13-22 SENEGALESE MUREX, *Siratus senegalensis* Gmelin; West Africa; 2½ inches. An uncommon species.

13-36

13-37

13-38

13-39

13-40

13-41

13-42

13-43

13-44

13-45

13-46

13-47

13-48

13-49

13-50

13-51

13-52

13-53

14-1

14-2

13-23 ZAMBO'S MUREX, *Homalocantha zamboi* Burch; Philippines; 2½ inches; a white shell with thickened, bladelike spines. (Pl. 150.)

13-24 SCORPIO MUREX, *Homalocantha scorpio* Linné; Indo-Pacific; 2 to 2½ inches; somewhat variable in coloration, from black to pure white.

13-25 BLACK MUREX, *Muricanthus nigritus* Philippi; west Mexico; 3 to 6 inches; white with black markings. A well known shell; imported and offered to tourists in many parts of the world. (Pl. 10.)

13-26 ROOT MUREX, *Muricanthus radix* Gmelin; west Panama to Ecuador; 3 to 4 inches; similar to preceding but with a smaller and heavier shell. (Pl. 38.)

13-27 CLAVUS MUREX, *Pterynotus elongatus* Lightfoot; Indo-Pacific; 2 to 3½ inches; a cream-colored shell somewhat resembling a key in shape, hence the name *Murex clavus* Lamarck, applied years after that of Lightfoot. (Pl. 73.)

13-28 WINGED MUREX, *Ocinebrellus euryp-teron* Reeve; off Japan; 2 to 2½ inches; an attractive species, brown with cream. (Pl. 11.)

13-29 VOKES' MUREX, *Pteropurpura vokesae* Emerson; off California coast; 2 to 2½ inches; similar to the preceding but with wings larger and with lacy scalation.

13-30 FOLIATED THORN-MUREX, *Ceratostoma foliata* Gmelin; Alaska to California; 2 to 3 inches; somewhat similar to the preceding, but coloration variable; lip with a large, projecting tooth, believed to be used in feeding.

13-31 SANTA ROSA MUREX, *Maxwellia santarosana* Dall; off California coast; 1½ to 2 inches; an uncommon species with low, reddish varices. (Pl. 27.)

13-32 MAGELLANIC TROPHON, *Trophon geversianus* Pallas; occurs along the extreme southern coast of South America from Chile to the Falklands; 2 to 3 inches. Also known as *Trophon magellanicus* Gmelin, a later name. (Pl. 91.)

13-33 BEEBE'S TROPHON, *Austrotrophon beebei* Hertlein and Strong; west Mexico; 2 to 3 inches; a deep-water species originally collected by William Beebe on an oceanographic expedition and named in his honor.

13-34 CATALINA TROPHON, *Austrotrophon catalinensis* Oldroyd; off Southern California; 2 to 3½ inches; a striking shell with bladelike varices. Formerly confused with a tiny shell of similar form, *Boreotrophon triangulatus* Carpenter. (Pl. 152.)

13-35 MURICATE THORN-DRUPE, *Acanthina muricata* Broderip; Mexico to Ecuador; 2 to 4 inches; largest species of its genus, which has a well developed projecting denticle on the lip. (Pls. 130, 137.)

13-36 COVERED CYMIA, *Cymia tecta* Wood; west Central America to Ecuador; 1½ to 2½

inches; an interesting uniform tan shell with a raised ridge in the columella; operculum therefore V-shaped to conform to the shape of the aperture.

13-37 KNOBBED PURPLE, *Thais armigera* Link; Indo-Pacific; 2½ to 4 inches; shell with large and evenly spaced knobs. All *Thais* possess a dye-producing mechanism. (Pl. 152.)

13-38 RINGED PURPLE, *Thais cingulata* Linné; South Africa; 1 to 1½ inches; a striking shell with raised spiral ribs. Uncommon.

13-39 RED-MOUTH ROCK SHELL, *Thais haemastoma* Linné; Mediterranean Sea, eastern and western Atlantic; 2 to 4½ inches; gray to yellowish brown, aperture salmon-pink. A common, quite variable species with several subspecies. (Pl. 159.)

13-40 KIOSK PURPLE, *Thais kiosquiformis* Duclos; common along the west coast of Mexico southward to Peru; 1½ to 2 inches; a gray or brown shell. (Pl. 141.)

13-41 PRINCELY PURPLE, *Thais persica* Linné; Indo-Pacific; 3 to 4½ inches; a large, smooth species with a wide, flaring aperture; brown with fine spiral rows of dots.

13-42 OPEN-MOUTHED PURPLE, *Concholepas concholepas* Bruguière; Peru to Chile; 2 to 6 inches; the smaller specimens are quite scaly; aperture is very expanded; appearance of a clam shell; operculum quite small. (Pls. 2, 133.)

THE LATIAXIS AND CORAL SNAILS
(Family Magilidae)

These attractive and delicately sculptured snails are found associated with hard or soft corals. Most are parasitic feeders and have lost their radulae. The shells are commonly alabaster white, less commonly pink or yellow. The Papery Rapa Shell lives completely embedded within the stalks of soft corals.

13-43 MAWE'S LATIAXIS, *Latiaxis mawae* Griffith and Pidgeon; deep water off Japan; 2 to 2½ inches; shell white with a partially "unwound" body whorl in large specimens. Formerly a collector's item, today they are more readily obtainable. (Pl. 26.)

13-44 PILSBRY'S LATIAXIS, *Latiaxis pilsbryi* Hirase; deep water off Japan and Formosa; 1½ inches; a choice species similar to the preceding but with a flattened, depressed spire. (Pl. 27.)

13-45 DEBURGH'S LATIAXIS, *Latiaxis deburghiae* Reeve; off Japan; 1 inch; small, uncommon species; white, yellow, or pinkish.

13-46 KAWAMURA'S LATIAXIS, *Latiaxis kawamurai* Kuroda; deep water off Japan; 1½ inches. Described rather recently; uncommon. (Pl. 26.)

13-47 KIRA'S LATIAXIS, *Latiaxis kirana* Kuroda; off Japan; 1½ inches; an attractive shell with numerous spinous ribs. (Pl. 27.)

14-3

14-4

14-6

14-5

14-7

14-8

15-1

15-2

15-3

15-4

15-5

15-6

15-7

15-8

15-9

15-10

15-11

13-48 LISCHKE'S LATIAXIS, *Latiaxis lischkeanus* Dunker; Japan; 1½ to 2 inches; with a row of petal-like processes around the spire, surface with uniform short spines; a handsome species. (Pl. 26.)

13-49 JAPANESE LATIAXIS, *Latiaxis japonica* Dunker; Japan; 1½ to 2 inches; similar to the preceding but with two rows of pointed spines on spire. While many species of latiaxis occur in Japanese waters, this one's specific name cites the country of origin.

13-50 EUGENIA'S LATIAXIS, *Latiaxis eugeniae* Bernardi; Japan; 1½ to 2 inches; elegant shell lacking spines but with spiral striae. Uncommon.

13-51 TOP LATIAXIS, *Latiaxis gyratus* Hinds; Formosa; 1½ to 2 inches; similar to the preceding species but with an angled keel on the whorls.

13-52 VIOLET CORAL SNAIL, *Coralliophila violacea* Kiener; Indo-Pacific; ¾ to 1½ inches; shell cream, often eroded or encrusted; aperture brilliant violet. A common coral-reef-dwelling species. (Pls. 120, 121.)

13-53 PAPERY RAPA, *Rapa rapa* Linné; Indo-Pacific; 3 inches; a rather thin, creamy yellow snail with a flat spire and wide flaring aperture; lives embedded in stalks of soft corals.

14. Superfamily Buccinacea

THE FALSE WHELKS AND OTHER BUCCINIDS (Family Buccinidae)

This is a large family of carnivorous snails. Many species are commonly referred to as whelks. There are about two thousand species, placed in many genera. Their distribution is practically cosmopolitan, representatives occurring in the polar seas as well as in tropical waters. The operculum, which is lacking in some species, is horny.

14-1 RIBBED MACRON, *Macron aethiops* Reeve; west Mexico; 2 to 3 inches; a white shell with velvety green periostracum. As in *Thais cingulata,* the sculpture is variable, and a shell may be heavily corded to smooth with little ribbing present. In the past, the various morphological forms were considered different species. (Pl. 86.)

THE CROWN AND TRUE WHELK SHELLS (Family Melongenidae)

This family contains some of the best known and most familiar of gastropod shells. The King's Crown is found from Florida along the Gulf Coast to Mexico, with relatives in the Caribbean, Panamic, and Indo-Pacific Provinces. *Semifusus morio* has an unusual distribution, being found in Trinidad, Brazil, and West Africa. The genus *Busycon* is endemic to east America, being found from Cape Cod southward to eastern Mexico. A related genus, *Hemifusus,* lives in Japanese and East Asiatic waters. One of the largest living species of gastropods, *Syrinx aruanus,* the AUSTRALIAN BAND SHELL, is placed here. Occurring around the tropical northern half of the Australian continent, it often attains a length of 24 inches.

14-2 LEFT-HANDED WHELK or LIGHTNING WHELK, *Busycon contrarium* Conrad; North Carolina south to northern Mexico; 4 to 18 inches. Small specimens are often marked with dark brown axial stripes resembling fulgurations or lightning streaks; large individuals are usually light gray or white. The animal is jet black. This is the only common sinistral, or left-handed, marine gastropod in the world. (Pl. 87.)

14-3 WEST INDIAN CROWN SHELL, *Melongena melongena* Linné; Caribbean area; 3 to 6 inches; a heavy, solid shell with a few knobby spines present. Shell brown; occasionally a specimen has a white median band.

14-4 KING'S CROWN, *Melongena corona* Gmelin; Florida to Mexico; 2 to 6 inches. A familiar Florida shell, long used in the shell novelty trade or as souvenirs. This species is a very variable one, and a collection could be formed of specimens depicting different sizes, shapes, coloration, and spinal development. (Pl. 153.)

THE HORSE CONCHS AND TULIP SHELLS (Family Fasciolariidae)

This family contains the other contender for the title of "World's Largest Snail," *Pleuroploca gigantea* Kiener, the HORSE CONCH, which occurs from North Carolina to Mexico. Although a specimen of 24 inches is a rarity, the shell is much more solid and much heavier than that of the Australian Band Shell. These carnivores have a large, horny operculum that seals the aperture when the animal is withdrawn.

14-5 BANDED TULIP, *Fasciolaria hunteria* Perry; North Carolina to Florida; 2 to 4 inches. Another common species along the Florida coasts; live shells are gray with darker spiral lines; beachworn shells are dull and orange in color. Though the species was long known as *Fasciolaria distans* Lamarck, Perry's name has priority by eleven years. (Pl. 87.)

14-6 BRANHAM'S TULIP, *Fasciolaria branhamae* Rehder and Abbott; trawled off Texas and northern Mexico to Yucatán; 4 to 5 inches; similar to the preceding but larger, with a produced, brown-stained canal and darker spiral banding. Not common. Named for Mrs. Hugh Branham, a Florida collector.

14-7 DUMPY TULIP, *Paralagena smaragdula* Linné; Indo-Pacific; 2 to 2½ inches; brown with fine white banding. A widespread species. (Pl. 169.)

15-12

15-13

15-16

15-15

15-14

15-17

15-18

15-19

15-20

14-8 ZEBRA THORN-SHELL, *Opeatostoma pseudodon* Burrow, better known as *Leucozonia cingulata* Lamarck (a later name); west Mexico south to Peru; 1 to 2½ inches; a strikingly handsome shell, white with spiral bands of black or brown. Aperture with a long, spikelike tooth, similar to that in *Acanthina,* used to wedge apart the valves of clams. (Pls. 81, 156.)

15. Superfamily Volutacea

THE OLIVE SHELLS (Family Olividae)

Olive shells are a family of cylindrical snails with highly glazed shells. They occur in sandy or mud bottoms in warm waters of the world. There are some two hundred species of *Olivella, Ancilla,* and other related genera, but only about eighty species of true *Oliva,* which lack an operculum.

15-1 WHITE-CALLUSED ANCILLA, *Ancilla albocallosa* Lischke; Japan; 2½ inches; shell of richly contrasting colors, body whorl purplish with a chocolate brown area above, base with brown and white bands, apex covered with a white callus. (Pl. 128.)

15-2 IREDALE'S ANCILLA, *Ancilla velesiana* Iredale; northeastern Australia; 2½ to 3 inches; similar to above but larger and lighter in weight; spire not callused, but glossy and chestnut brown in color. (Pl. 128.)

15-3 TENT OLIVE or ROYAL PURPLE OLIVE, *Oliva porphyria* Linné, west Mexico to Panama; 3 to 5 inches; a superb species, beautifully marked with chocolate brown on a pink background. (Pls. 162, 163.)

15-4 MOOR OLIVE, *Oliva vidua* Lamarck (also known as *Oliva maura* Lamarck; Indo-Pacific; 2 to 2½ inches; very variable in coloration. In some localities the shell is olive gray with black markings; some shells are solid black; others may be entirely orange, olive, ochraceous, brown, or mottled.

15-5 LIGNARIA OLIVE, *Oliva lignaria* Marrat; Western Pacific; 2 to 2½ inches; another species that is variably colored, ivory, solid orange, solid brown, or white. The spire is covered with a callus, hence the name *Oliva cryptospira* Ford, which is a synonym. (Pl. 110.)

THE MITER SHELLS (Family Mitridae)

A large family; some six hundred species have been described, most of which are less than one inch in length. Most species occur in the Indo-Pacific Province. Several species closely resemble shells placed in other families; there are *Mitra* that resemble cones, olives, columbellids, buccinids, augers, and others. The common name, miter, was derived from the shape of the shell, which resembles a bishop's miter. Ecclesiastical names have been bestowed on several species, such as *pontificalis, episcopalis, cardinalis, papalis,* to cite a few.

15-6 EPISCOPAL MITER, *Mitra mitra* Linné; Indo-Pacific; 3 to 5 inches; a handsome species, white with red or orange markings. (Pl. 128.)

15-7 PONTIFICAL MITER, *Mitra stictica* Link; Indo-Pacific; 2 to 2½ inches; similar to the preceding but with a row of pointed knobs on each whorl; red markings. Often with rows of punctures. (Pl. 86.)

15-8 POOR MITER, *Strigatella paupercula* Linné; Indo-Pacific; 1 inch; yellow with black axial stripes. (Pl. 168.)

15-9 RED-LINED MITER, *Tiara praestantissima* Röding; Indo-Pacific; 1 inch; white with raised spiral red-brown lines. (Pl. 168.)

15-10 VITTATE MITER, *Vexillum vittatum* Swainson; Western Pacific; 2½ inches; a very colorful shell with alternating bands of orange and white separated by a black line. Not common. (Pl. 128.)

THE CHANK SHELLS
(Family Turbinellidae)

15-10a West Indian Chank, *Turbinella angulatus* Lightfoot; northern Caribbean; 7 to 14 inches; shell ivory white with orange aperture. A heavy shell with large folds on the columella (shown in sectioned specimen, plate 56). Better known under the generic name *Xancus;* the generic name now in use, *Turbinella,* should not be confused with *Turbonilla,* which are minute pyram shells.

THE HARP SHELLS (Family Harpidae)

Harp shells are a small family of some eight living species. One species lives in the Panamic Province and another in West Africa. The remainder inhabit the Indo-Pacific Province. This is a group of snails that are capable of autotomy, or the breaking off of the posterior portion of the creeping foot if it is seized by an enemy. The shells possess numerous ribs or varices and are brightly colored, making them popular with collectors.

15-11 VENTRICOSE HARP, *Harpa major* Röding; Indian Ocean; 3 to 5 inches; shell with about a dozen strong ribs; pink and purplish brown with whorls of darker brown between the ribs. (Pls. 92, 161.)

15-12 MANY-RIBBED HARP, *Harpa costata* Linné; Mauritius; 3 to 4 inches; similar to the preceding but with thirty or more ribs; aperture yellow-orange. (Pls. 87, 136.)

THE VOLUTE SHELLS (Family Volutidae)

The volutes are a group of some two hundred

15-21

15-22

15-24

15-23

15-25

15-26

15-27

15-29

15-30

16-4

16-3

16-1

16-2

16-7

16-6

16-5

carnivorous species. Most occur in the tropics and are highly colored. An operculum occurs in the genus *Voluta* but is lacking in the other genera. In the nineteenth century, the volutes, together with the cones and cowries, were considered the "aristocracy" of sea shells. In the past, collectors vied to obtain rare or choice specimens. Today, many species of the formerly rare volutes are easily obtainable.

15-13 MUSIC VOLUTE, *Voluta musica* Linné; Caribbean area; 2 to 3½ inches; an attractive species, variable in shape and coloration; olive brown or orange, with spiral bands of darker markings that resemble a written musical score. (Pl. 170.)

15-14 HEBREW VOLUTE, *Voluta ebraea* Linné; Brazil; similar to the preceding but attains a larger size, occasionally 6 inches or more; the shell has brown markings on a cream background. The markings resemble Hebrew inscription, hence the name.

15-15 NOBLE VOLUTE, *Aulica nobilis* Lightfoot; Southeast Asia; 5 inches or larger; an attractive species, rectangular in outline and heavy for its size; markings variable but usually brown on a pinkish background.

15-16 AULICA VOLUTE, *Aulica aulica* Lightfoot; Sulu Sea; 4 to 5 inches; a Philippine species, with red markings on a pinkish background, or solid red in coloration. Uncommon. (Pl. 127.)

15-17 BEDNALL'S VOLUTE, *Volutoconus bednalli* Brazier; northern Australia; 4 to 5 inches; a beautiful cream shell with brown or purplish brown markings. Rather rare and a choice collector's item. (Pl. 171.)

15-18 YELLOW VOLUTE, *Aulica flavicans* Gmelin; northern Australia; 3 to 4 inches; quite variable in both shape and coloration. Previously, several forms were recognized as distinct species but are now considered local variants.

15-19 RUSSET VOLUTE, *Cymbiolacca complexa* Iredale; Queensland, Australia; 2½ inches; shell handsomely marked with brick red bands and blackish dots on a reddish background. (Pl. 127.)

15-20 IMPERIAL VOLUTE, *Aulica imperialis* Lamarck; Sulu Sea; 3 to 10 inches; a large and striking shell with a row of projecting spines around the spire; nucleus large and purplish brown in color, shell cream to pink overlaid with brown markings. (Pl. 68.)

15-21 ELLIOT'S VOLUTE, *Amoria ellioti* Sowerby; northwest Australia; 2 to 3 inches; a handsome zebra-striped volute, background cream with axial lines of chocolate brown. Not common. (Pl. 172.)

15-22 WAVY VOLUTE, *Amoria undulata* Lamarck; southern Australia; 2½ to 3½ inches; a pinkish shell with axial brown lines that waver or appear to ripple over the surface of the shell. Rather common. (Pl. 165.)

15-23 MACANDREW'S VOLUTE, *Amoria macandrewi* Sowerby; southwest Australia; 2 inches; somewhat similar to the preceding but a smaller species with more delicate coloration. Some specimens have an opalescent sheen. Rare. (Pl. 168.)

15-24 ZEBRA VOLUTE, *Amoria zebra* Leach; northeastern Australia; 2 inches. The typical form is easily identified; smaller than Elliot's Volute, it is rather similar, with evenly spaced brown stripes on a cream background. The form *A. z. lineata* Leach, the Lineated Volute, from the same general area, attains a slightly larger size and is very variable in pattern: dark purplish brown, crowded brown lines, interrupted lineation, solid orange, or white; aperture usually stained a dark purple. (Pl. 172.)

15-25 JUNONIA or JUNO'S VOLUTE, *Scaphella junonia* Shaw; southeastern United States, with closely related forms occurring around the Gulf of Mexico; 4 to 5 inches; strikingly marked with squarish black spots on a cream-colored shell; aperture and lower columella light orange. The most popular American volute.

15-26 DUFRESNE'S VOLUTE, *Zidona dufresnei* Donovan; Brazil and Uruguay; 3 to 8 inches; a glazed orange or pinkish shell, often brown stained. Many local variants exist, of which the most interesting are those with a long callus extending from the spine. Better known as *Zidona angulata* Swainson, a later name. (Pl. 28.)

15-27 OLLA VOLUTE, *Cymbium olla* Linné; southern Spain, Portugal, northwest Africa; 3½ to 5 inches; a brownish shell, the only representative of the volute family occurring on the coast of continental Europe. (Pl. 88.)

15-28 NEPTUNE'S VOLUTE, *Cymbium pepo* Lightfoot; West Africa; 4 to 9 inches; similar to the preceding but attaining a larger size. Better known as *Cymbium neptunei* Gmelin, a later name. (Pls. 25, 89.)

15-29 GEORGINA VOLUTE, *Melo georginae* Griffith and Pidgeon; Queensland, Australia; 3 to 10 inches; an Australian species of considerable variation during growth and in coloration; small specimens are usually cream with orange markings or orange with brown markings, as is the one shown here.

THE GEM SHELLS (Family Marginellidae)

The gem or little margin shells are a family of some two hundred species of rather small, highly polished shells similar to cowries. Most of the species are quite small; among the largest are the GREAT MARGIN SHELLS, *Bullata bullata* Linné, from Brazil, which attains a size of 3½ inches, and PRINGLE'S FALSE VOLUTE, *Afrivoluta pringlei* Tomlin, from South Africa, which attains a size of 5 inches. As the name implies, the latter species was formerly thought to be a volute. An operculum is lacking. Most species

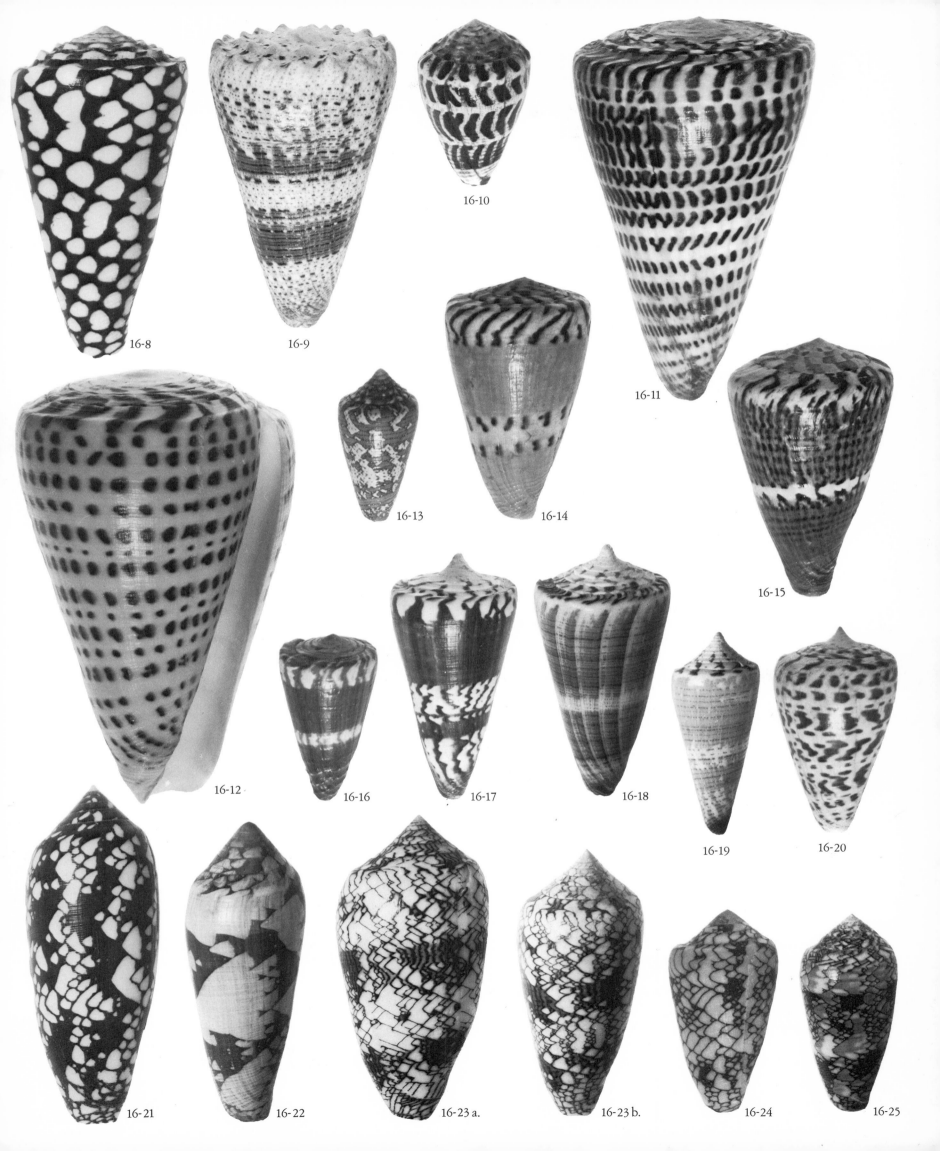

16-8

16-9

16-10

16-11

16-12

16-13

16-14

16-15

16-16

16-17

16-18

16-19

16-20

16-21

16-22

16-23 a.

16-23 b.

16-24

16-25

are tropical, but some occur in temperate waters.

15-30 BELTED MARGIN SHELL, *Persicula cingulata* Dillwyn; West Africa; 1 inch; a handsome glazed shell, cream with brown banding. Not common.

16. Superfamily Conacea

THE TURRIDS (Family Turridae)

This is a large family of highly evolved snails. Most of the twelve hundred known species are found in rather deep water. Also the majority are small. Turrids occur in many different shapes, from highly attenuated shells with elongated canals, to short, dumpy, globular ones. A characteristic found in virtually all of them is an opened posterior canal. In some genera it is reduced to a notch or slight indentation, but in the majority of species the canal is excavated. Some species lack an operculum; if one is present, it is horny.

16-1 CRISPA TURRID, *Turris crispa* Lamarck; Indo-Pacific; 2 to 6 inches, giving it the greatest length of any living turrid; shell is quite variable in size and markings, but usually displays dark markings on a cream-colored shell. (Pl. 12.)

16-2 BABYLON TURRID, *Turris babylonia* Linné; Indo-Pacific; 2 to 3 inches; a handsome shell similar to the preceding but with squarish black or chocolate markings. (Pl. 13.)

16-3 COSMO'S TURRID, *Gemmula congener cosmoi* Sykes; off Japan; 2 to 2½ inches; a pretty shell, bluish white with a fine red-brown line at the suture. Related forms occur throughout the Indo-Pacific. (Pl. 140.)

16-4 KADERLY'S TURRID, *Comitas kaderlyi* Lischke; Japan to the Philippines; 2½ to 3½ inches; a chocolate brown and white shell. Not common. (Pl. 13.)

16-5 SOUTHERN TURRID, *Nihonia australis* Roissy; China Sea area; at 3 to 4 inches, a rather large, thin shell with a deeply incised canal. The specific name does not indicate an Australian distribution: "australis" means "southern." (Pl. 13.)

16-6 ELEGANT STAR TURRET, *Cochlespira elegans* Dall; Caribbean in deep water; 2 to 2½ inches; an elegant and beautiful shell, straw-colored or yellowish; its delicate sculpture consists of two spiral rows of tiny spines that cause collectors to vie for specimens. Rare. (Pl. 87.)

16-7 MIRACULOUS THATCHERIA, *Thatcheria mirabilis* Sowerby; Japan and Formosa; 2½ to 5 inches; straw-colored, occasionally pinkish. The largest of the family (though the Crispa Turrid attains a greater length). In general form, it looks like a monstrosity of a cone or of some other shell. In the past many authorities considered it just that—a freak of some common species of gastropod. Specimens were very rare

in collections until the late 1940s; today they are inexpensive and can be obtained quite easily. (Pl. 90.)

THE CONE SHELLS (Family Conidae)

This is a family of some four hundred species, most of which occur in the Indo-Pacific Marine Province. About fifty species occur in the Americas, and one in the Mediterranean. The aperture is reduced to a very long, narrow slit, and the operculum is very thin. Most species feed upon marine worms and a few are known to kill and eat fish. The cones have developed a virulent venom for "stinging" their prey, or for defense. Actually they bite, and the poison is injected through a hollow tooth, much like that of venomous snakes or spiders.

16-8 MARBLED CONE, *Conus marmoreus* Linné; Indo-Pacific; 3 to 4 inches; a handsome species with white dots or blotches on a black background; aperture white or pinkish. Spire coronate with evenly spaced, raised nodules. (Pls. 100, 170.)

16-9 IMPERIAL CONE, *Conus imperialis* Linné; Indo-Pacific generally; 2 to 3 inches; color variable but usually a white shell with bands or zones of olive brown, overlaid with black dots. Coronations on spire more conspicuous than in preceding species.

16-10 HEBREW CONE, *Conus ebraeus* Linné; Indo-Pacific; 1/2 to 2 inches; shell white with black dots. One of the smaller, but also one of the best known species, as it occurs in shallow water over a large range. Large specimens are popular with collectors. (Pl. 164.)

16-11 LETTERED CONE, *Conus litteratus* Linné; Indo-Pacific; 3 to 5 inches; a variable shell, ground color may be white, yellow, or orange, with dots or dashes of purplish brown or black. Base of shell tapered and with purplish stain. (Pl. 100.)

16-12 LEOPARD CONE, *Conus leopardus* Hwass; Indo-Pacific; 4 to 9 inches; often confused with the Lettered Cone, but has a truncated base that is always white; no purplish stain. Shell white or cream with brown dots, often edged with slate blue. Intermediate rows of fine russet dots. Not the largest species of cone, but the heaviest in weight.

16-13 MATCHLESS CONE, *Conus cedonulli* Linné; Lesser Antilles; 1½ to 2 inches; this handsome shell is cream with brown or ochraceous markings resembling embroidery work. One of the cones that caused spirited bidding at European shell auctions in the past. Its name *cedonulli*, "I yield to none," is appropriate. Rather rare. (Pl. 165.)

16-14 WEASEL CONE, *Conus mustelinus* Hwass; Indo-Pacific; 2 to 2½ inches; a greenish or yellowish shell with two zones of white, over-

16-26

16-27

16-28

16-29

16-30

16-31

16-32

16-33

16-34

16-35

16-36

16-37

16-38

16-39

17-1

17-2

17-3

18-1

18-2

laid with black markings. Not common. (Pl. 101.)

16-15 CAPTAIN'S CONE, *Conus capitaneus* Linné; Indo-Pacific; 2 to 3 inches; similar to the preceding but larger and more angulate; pigmented zones ochraceous or olivaceous with numerous black markings. (Pl. 101.)

16-16 LITHOGRAPH CONE, *Conus lithoglyphus* Hwass; Indo-Pacific; 1½ to 2½ inches; shell red-brown with contrasting white zones. A handsome cone; formerly uncommon.

16-17 GENERAL CONE, *Conus generalis* Linné; Indo-Pacific; 2 to 3½ inches; another species that may be very variable in pattern; from light orange to black, usually with two or three white zones.

16-18 MALDIVE CONE, *Conus maldivus* Hwass; Indian Ocean; 2 to 2½ inches; often confused with the preceding, the Maldive Cone is more somberly marked; red-brown on a white shell.

16-19 A color phase of the Maldive Cone (16-18) occurring in the Red Sea. Shell very smooth, with markings of yellow or orange. (Pl. 101.)

16-20 ALPHABET CONE, *Conus spurius* Gmelin; Gulf of Mexico and Caribbean; 2 to 3 inches. Quite variable; Florida specimens have brown markings on a cream shell, while those from further south have brown, black, or orange markings on a white shell. (Pl. 164.)

16-21 COURTLY CONE, *Conus aulicus* Linné; Indo-Pacific; 4 to 6 inches; shaped more like an olive shell, this species has white tent markings on a brown or russet shell; aperture yellow or orange stained. Not common. (Pls. 101, 165, 166.)

16-22 EPISCOPAL CONE, *Conus episcopus* Hwass; Indo-Pacific; 2 to 3½ inches; similar to the preceding, and usually marked with small tents. The variant shown is a rare one in which the white tents have coalesced into large white areas. (Pl. 101.)

16-23 TEXTILE CONE, *Conus textile* Linné; Indo-Pacific; 2 to 4 inches; one of the commonest of the family. Very variable in markings; usually with white tents on an orange background. The East African form shown on the left has more white areas. (Pls. 101, 166.) Novices frequently mistake this species for its larger relative, the GLORY-OF-THE-SEA CONE, *Conus gloriamaris* Chemnitz.

16-24 PENNIFORM CONE, *Conus pennaceus* Hwass; Indo-Pacific; 2 to 3 inches; another species that is rather variable in pattern; usually white tents on a chocolate brown background. Specimen shown is from Saudi Arabia and has much of the brown replaced by white tents.

16-25 PRELATE CONE, *Conus praelatus* Hwass; Indian Ocean; 2 to 2½ inches; another of the tent cones, in this species the white tents may be suffused with blue. Not common. (Pl. 101.)

16-26 SPECTRAL CONE, *Conus spectrum* Linné; Western Pacific; 1½ inches; shell white with tan, brown, or black markings; markings variable, often fanciful designs.

16-27 FIG CONE, *Conus figulinus* Linné; Indo-Pacific; 2 to 4 inches; a rich brown or chestnut-colored shell with spiral lines of chocolate; aperture white. Shell covered with a heavy tenacious periostracum in life. (Pls. 101, 170.)

16-28 BETULINE CONE, *Conus betulinus* Linné; Indo-Pacific; 3 to 6 inches; a pyriform cone, orange or yellow with a pattern of spiral rows of dots and dashes which may be black, black alternating with white, red-brown, or slate. Spire with alternating dark and light squarish spots. (Pls. 80, 100.)

16-29 GARTERED CONE, *Conus genuanus* Linné; West Africa; 1 to 3 inches; a strikingly beautiful shell, olive or olive brown with spiral rows of alternating brown and white checks; white areas often with a dark central dot. One of the most popular shells; not common. (Pl. 164.)

16-30 BUBBLE CONE, *Conus bullatus* Linné; Indo-Pacific; 2 to 3 inches; another handsome species; shell varies from orange to solid red in color; aperture cream or orange. Although distributed over a wide range, it is not common. (Pl. 101.)

16-31 FLY-SPECKED CONE, *Conus stercusmuscarum* Linné; Ceylon and Western Pacific; 1½ to 2½ inches; shell white with brown or black markings. Markings may be few, resembling fly specks, or numerous. Fairly common. (Pl. 164.)

16-32 STRIATE CONE, *Conus striatus* Linné; Indo-Pacific; 2 to 4 inches; quite variably marked; background may be white or suffused with pink, violet, or orange; markings brown, black, or gray. This species is piscivorous, "stings" and ingests small fish. A common species. (Pl. 165.)

16-33 CHESTNUT CONE, *Conus coccineus* Gmelin; Western Pacific; 1 to 2½ inches; another handsome species. Faded or beachworn specimens are ochraceous or yellow-brown; live-taken specimens are a deep chestnut brown; a white median band is usually present. (Pl. 101.)

16-34 SULCATE CONE, *Conus sulcatus* Hwass; Western Pacific; 2 to 4 inches; a distinctive shell; body whorl with numerous raised spiral ribs. Specimens from Japan and China are white or pale buff; those from the Philippines are buff or red-brown and with a smoother shell. (Pl. 140.)

THE AUGER SHELLS
(Family Terebridae)

These colorful mollusks form a group of long, tapered shells that somewhat resemble the turret shells (6-1); however, the aperture is elliptical in the auger shells, and the shell is much heavier and more solid. The horny operculum is clawlike. About three hundred species are known, many of which are less than one inch long. The largest species is the MARLINSPIKE, *Terebra maculata* Linné, of the Indo-Pacific. It commonly attains 6 to 8 inches in length, although specimens measuring 10 to 12 inches in length are known. Like the cones, auger shells possess a poison gland and are carnivorous, feeding on worms.

16-35 DIMIDIATE AUGER, *Terebra dimidiata* Linné; Indo-Pacific; 6 inches; shell is a rich orange with white markings.

16-36 SUBULATE AUGER, *Terebra subulata* Linné; Indo-Pacific; 6 inches; shell cream or white with squarish brown spots; two rows on each whorl, and three rows visible on the body whorl. (Pl. 12.)

16-37 AREOLATE AUGER, *Terebra areolata* Lamarck; Indo-Pacific; 6 inches; shell similar to *T. subulata* Linné but has three rows of spots on each whorl and four rows on the body whorl.

16-38 CRENULATE AUGER, *Terebra crenulata* Linné; Indo-Pacific; 6 inches; shell with a row of projecting nodes at the suture of each whorl. Shell gray when small, white or ivory when large, with fine red-brown markings. (Pl. 12.)

16-39 TRISERIATE AUGER, *Terebra triseriata* Gray; Western Pacific; 5 inches; an elongate tapered shell of striking design. Shells beaded at the sutures, and with spiral threads below the rows of beads. Color solid honey orange. Large specimens are collector's items. (Pls. 12, 24.)

Subclass Opisthobranchia

The opisthobranchs are a separate subclass of snails in which the heart is located behind the gills. Gills may be external, plumelike processes. Both sexes are present in the same individual. Many opisthobranchs possess only a rudimentary shell, or have lost the shell entirely. The bubble shells, however, have a large, flaring external shell. The operculum is lacking in adults.

Order Tectibranchia

17. Superfamily Bullacea

THE BUBBLE SHELLS (Family Bullidae)

These shells are widely distributed in warm waters. Largely carnivorous, these snails possess fragile shells which are often very thin and papery and offer little protection against predators. The animal itself is usually large and beautifully colored. Normally the animal is too large to draw into the shell.

THE HYDATINA BUBBLES
(Family Hydatinidae)

These are among the larger of the bubble shells, and their thin shells are marked with contrasting colors.

17-1 WHITE-BANDED BUBBLE, *Hydatina albocincta* van der Hoeven; Japan; 1 to 2½ inches; shell richly adorned with zones of deep chocolate and white or cream. The shell is not common in collections. (Pl. 160.)

17-2 ZONATE BUBBLE, *Hydatina zonata* Lightfoot; Indo-Pacific; 1 to 1½ inches; shell cream with two zones of chocolate lines. Uncommon. (Pl. 171.)

THE CANOE SHELLS
(Family Scaphandridae)

The canoe shells belong to a family in which the shells look tapered or scoop-shaped. The animals are large. They are carnivorous and feed voraciously on other snails. Powerful digestive organs enable them to devour and absorb sizable prey.

17-3 WOOD-GRAINED CANOE SHELL, *Scaphander lignarius* Linné; Europe; 2 to 2½ inches. As the name implies, the surface of the shell is covered with numerous fine lines, resembling the grain in certain kinds of wood such as oak. (Pl. 67.)

Order Pteropoda

18. Superfamily Cavoliniacea

THE CAVOLINA SEA BUTTERFLIES
(Family Cavoliniidae)

The sea butterflies are a world-wide group of small, thin-shelled marine snails with lobelike processes on the mantle that they use to propel themselves through the water. It is this swimming motion that has been responsible for their common name, sea butterflies.

18-1 WAVY CLIO, *Clio recurvum* Children; pelagic in Atlantic and Indo-Pacific; about 1 inch in length; a thin, transparent shell with rippled transverse ridges. Shell resembles a space capsule except that it is laterally compressed. (Pl. 31.)

18-2 THREE-TOOTHED CAVOLINE, *Cavolina tridentata* Forskål; pelagic world-wide; ½ to 1 inch; shell thin, often golden or metallic bronze in color. (Pl. 31.)

Subclass Pulmonata

Pulmonates are mostly terrestrial snails which have developed lungs and live on land. A number of seemingly typical marine shells are placed here because anatomically they are air breathers.

19. Superfamily Siphonariacea

THE FALSE LIMPETS
(Family Siphonariidae)

These shells resemble the true limpets (2-7). Both have a similar looking muscle scar inside the shell. In the true limpets there is a gap in the scar at the anterior end, while in the false limpets it is at one side.

19-1 LATTICED FALSE LIMPET, *Siphonaria laciniosa* Linné; Western Pacific; 1 inch; a prettily marked shell, brown with eight bluish ribs; interior brown with a cream-colored margin.

Class Polyplacophora

Order Isoplacophora

The chitons or coat-of-mail shells comprise an order of about six hundred living species. Basically they are a limpetlike animal with a shell of eight plates held together by a leathery encircling girdle.

To prepare chitons as cabinet specimens, you must tie them on tongue depressors or similar plastic or wooden strips and dry them or place them in alcohol. If removed from the rock, they curl up like an armadillo or a sow bug. Many collectors, however, prefer to disarticulate their specimens, clean them in a weak chlorine solution, and then glue the eight valves together in a more or less natural position.

THE MOPALID CHITONS
(Family Mopaliidae)

This is a group of fairly large-sized chitons, often with bristly integument on the girdle. The valves are rather smooth and with little or no sculpture. The interior of the valves is often brightly colored, such as turquoise, blue, or rose tinted. The mopalids reach their zenith on the west coast of North America.

20-1 HIND'S MOPALIA, *Mopalia hindsi* Sowerby; Alaska to California; 2 to 3 inches. As can be seen from the illustrated specimen, the surrounding girdle is flat and leathery and covered with very short hairs. The eight valves are keeled or ridged at their midpoint. This area is often eroded or abraded because of the chiton's habit of clambering over and under slabs of rock. Girdle dull brown, valves dark green, and the interior of the valves white. (Pl. 114.)

20-2 HAIRY CHITON, *Mopalia ciliata* Sowerby; Alaska to California; 1 to 2 inches. This species is green, olive, orange, red-brown, brown, or mottled in a combination of these colors. Inside the valves are white with a tint of rose at the center. This specimen has had the girdle removed. (Pl. 114.)

20-3 MOSSY MOPALIA, *Mopalia muscosa* Gould; Alaska to Lower California; 1 to 2 inches; valves are finely sculptured with wavy lines and black, gray, olive, brown, or orange in color. The Mossy Mopalia gets its name from the long hairy tufts covering its girdle, which was removed from this specimen. (Pl. 114.)

Order Teleoplacophora

THE TYPICAL CHITONS
(Family Chitonidae)

These chitons usually have the encircling girdle composed of scales, much like reptile skin. Interior of the valves is usually blue-green. The spiny chitons (genus *Acanthopleura*), which are also placed in this family because of technical characters, resemble the mopalia chitons at first glance.

20-4 SPINY CHITON, *Acanthopleura echinata* Barnes; Peru and Chile; 3 to 5 inches. A remarkable shell, endemic to the west coast of South America. The girdle is composed of long black spines. However, the illustrated specimen has them covered with a nulliporal growth (calcareous algae). The valves are gray-black, often covered with green or brown algae, and the interior is cream-colored with a red-brown blotch in the center of each valve. Not common. (Pl. 115.)

20-5 STOKES' CHITON, *Chiton stokesii* Broderip; west Mexico south to Ecuador; 3 inches; shell gray to blackish brown, with scaled girdle resembling snake skin. Interior a brilliant blue-green. (Pl. 114.)

Class Scaphopoda

THE SCAPHOPODS (Family Dentaliidae)

These are rather small, specialized mollusks with a tapered shell that is open at both ends. Commonly referred to as tusk or tooth shells, they are widely distributed around the world, inhabiting shallow bays, while some species are found at considerable depths in the oceans. Shells are smooth, annulated, or longitudinally ribbed. Two of the most highly colored species are shown here.

21-1 ELEPHANT TUSK SHELL, *Dentalium elephantinum* Linné; Western Pacific; 2½ to 4 inches; a ridged shell with rich green coloration over most of the surface, paling into white toward the smaller end. (Pl. 107.)

21-2 FORMOSAN MAROON TUSK, *Dentalium formosum* Adams and Reeve; Formosa; 2 to 3 inches; shell similar to the preceding but with

19-1

20-1

20-2

20-3

20-4

21-1

21-2

22-1

22-2

22-3

22-4

more numerous ribbing; coloration maroon, plum, and white. Uncommon. (Pl. 107.)

Class Bivalvia

Clams, scallops, and oysters are all mollusks consisting of two separate shells or valves hinged together by a muscular ligament. They comprise the second largest class of mollusks and are found in marine, brackish, or fresh-water habitats. Clams range from minute pinhead-sized species to the Giant Clam, which may weigh up to 600 pounds. They are headless, and most feed by filtering planktonic particles through their gills.

Order Filibranchia

22. Superfamily Arcacea

THE ARK SHELLS (Family Arcidae)

The arks are a family of elongate shells, usually with rather heavy raised ribs. In the ligamental area there is a row of interlocking file or toothlike projections in each valve; these serve as a further means of holding the two valves together. More than two hundred living species inhabit the seas of the world.

22-1 TWISTED ARK, *Trisidos tortuosa* Linné; Western Pacific; 2½ to 3½ inches. This is one of the oddest ark shells in shape; the anterior end is of normal development but the posterior is flared and twisted at an angle. Surface covered with fine ribs. Coloration variable, yellow and white, pinkish, or bright orange. (Pls. 66, 138.)

22-2 BEADED ARK, *Anadara granosa* Linné; Indo-Pacific; 2 to 3 inches. A white shell, covered with a brown periostracum in life. About eighteen large raised ribs, regularly beaded with closely spaced rounded beads. (Pl. 44.)

THE BITTERSWEET CLAMS
(Family Glycymeridae)

These bivalves are characterized by having circular disklike shells. In addition to the hinge, there are a number of raised toothlike projections, which serve as an additional means of keeping the two valves tightly shut.

22-3 UNEQUAL BITTERSWEET, *Glycymeris inaequalis* Sowerby; west Mexico to Peru; 2 inches; an attractive species, shell white with chocolate striping. Also known as *Glycymeris assimilis* Sowerby.

22-4 GIANT BITTERSWEET, *Glycymeris gigantea* Reeve; west Mexico and Central America; 3 to 4 inches; one of the largest species of the family; the shell is quite smooth, cream or tan with numerous brown markings.

23. Superfamily Pteriacea

THE TOOTHED TREE-OYSTERS
(Family Isognomonidae)

These form a small family of extremely flattened, brittle shells, usually found in clusters attached to aerial roots of mangroves and other trees inhabiting tropical mud flats.

23-1 WINGED TREE-OYSTER, *Isognomon isognomon* Linné; Western Pacific; 4 to 5 inches. A purplish gray shell, similar to the following, the hammer oysters, but differing in having the hinge area beveled and with about twenty grooves in each valve. Hence the vernacular name, "toothed." Interior of shell nacreous. (Pls. 3, 61, 139.)

THE HAMMER OYSTERS
(Family Malleidae)

These are a small group of elongate oysterlike bivalves with projections that give them the appearance of a pick or a hammer. There are about eight species, all of which are native to the Indo-Pacific.

23-2 COMMON HAMMER OYSTER, *Malleus malleus* Linné; Indo-Pacific; 4 to 6 inches in length; shell black or dark gray outside, interior tan with an area of the muscle scar silvery. A common species. (Pls. 3, 6.)

23-3 DISTORTED HAMMER OYSTER, *Malleus normalis* Lamarck; Western Pacific; 3 inches; shell semitranslucent, with fine brown dots. A species that usually lives embedded in certain kinds of sponges. (Pl. 3.)

THE PEARL OYSTERS AND WING OYSTERS (Family Pteriidae)

These differ from the true or edible oysters in that their shells have a nacreous or iridescent lining. The shell of the true oyster has a dull or porcellaneous interior. Pearls of commercial value grow inside the shells of this family. Pearls, however, can be produced by virtually any species of bivalve (and a number of gastropods have been known to develop them), but they are usually baroques or curios and seldom have much appeal as jewelry nor do they have commercial value.

23-4 BLACK-LIPPED PEARL OYSTER, *Pinctada margaritifera* Linné; Indo-Pacific; 4 to 10 inches; exterior variegated and variously colored; interior a deep silvery nacreous with a black border. While this species produces pearls, it has been harvested commercially for centuries for the mother-of-pearl. This is the mother-of-pearl of inlay work, buttons, jewelry, etc. In Japan, cultured pearls are grown in a similar

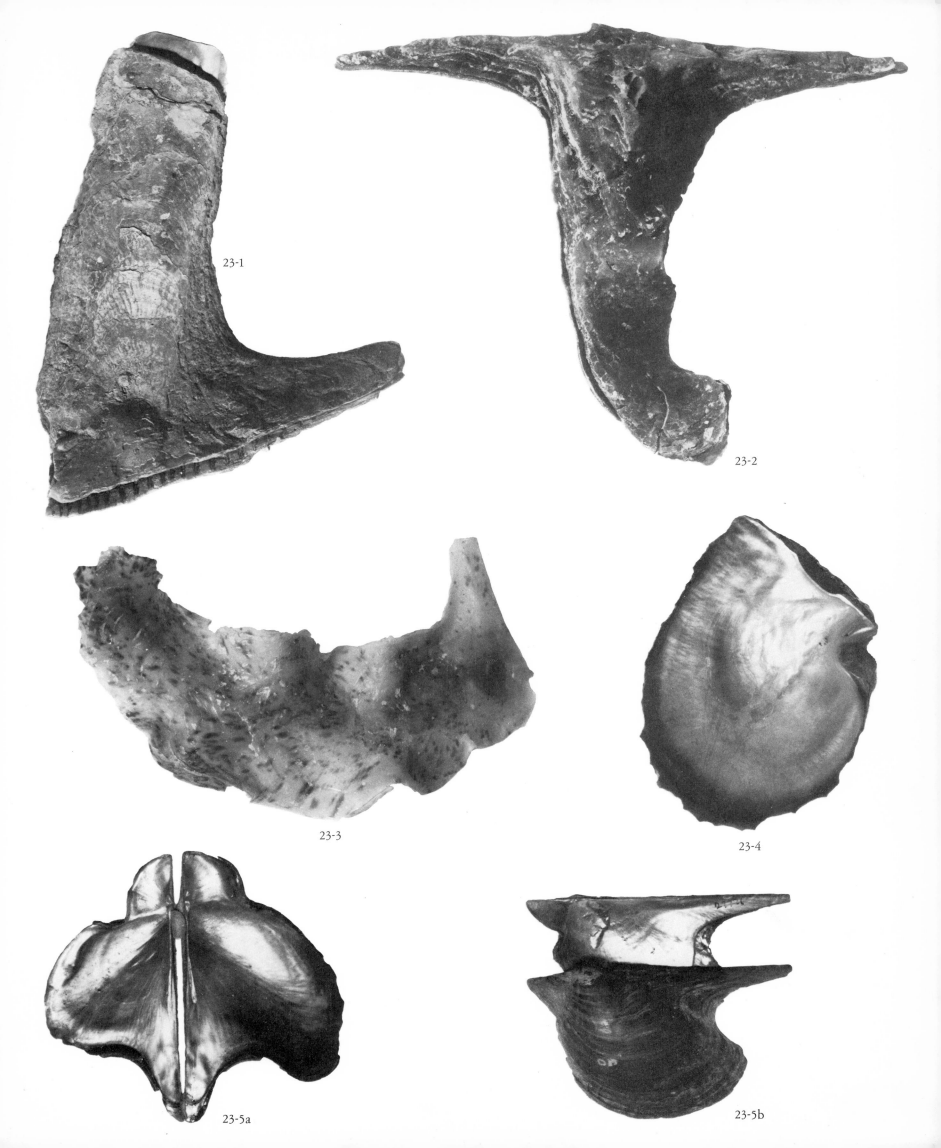

23-1

23-2

23-3

23-4

23-5a

23-5b

species, *Pinctada mertensi* Dunker, which attains a size of about 3 inches.

23-5a, b ATLANTIC WINGED OYSTER, *Pteria colymbus* Röding; southeast United States and West Indies; 1½ to 3 inches; exterior variable from black to green, interior with a silvery nacreous lining. The posterior extensions are thin, brittle, and easily broken.

THE PEN SHELLS (Family Pinnidae)

The pen shells are large, thin, flattened shells that are elongately triangular in outline. They live with the pointed end in the substrate and are anchored in place by numerous byssal threads. The ancient Mediterraneans gathered them and wove the "Golden Fleece" from byssal threads of *Pinna nobilis* Linné.

23-6 TERAMACHI'S PEN SHELL, *Atrina teramachii* Habe; Japan; 5 inches; shell pinkish orange with numerous filelike ridges covering the surface.

24. Superfamily Mytilacea

THE MUSSEL SHELLS
(Family Mytilidae)

Mussel shells are among the most abundant of mollusks. In many parts of the world they have long been used as food, though they are not a popular sea-food item in the United States. The shells are rather thin and in life are anchored in place by numerous threadlike guy wires. All live in marine or brackish water, and they should not be confused with the fresh-water mussels.

24-1 GREEN MUSSEL, *Mytilus viridis* Linné; Western Pacific; 2 to 3 inches; a striking shell, with the exterior a brilliant jade green in color, interior opalescent. (Pl. 122.)

25. Superfamily Pectinacea

THE PECTENS OR SCALLOPS
(Family Pectinidae)

These bivalves belong to a large family that is world-wide in distribution. There are several hundred species, among which are some of the most brilliantly colored bivalves. Many species are commercially fished, and scallops are an important sea-food item in many countries. Pectens are one of the most popular families with shell collectors.

25-1 LAURENT'S MOON SCALLOP, *Amusium laurenti* Gmelin; Gulf of Mexico; 2½ to 3½ inches; the flattened upper valve is red-brown or lavender and the curved lower one is white. A rather uncommon species that is occasionally taken by trawling.

25-2 LION'S PAW, *Lyropecten nodosus* Linné; Gulf of Mexico and Caribbean; 3 to 5 inches. The Lion's Paw has the surface covered with a few large ridgelike ribs and evenly spaced large nodes. The coloration is variable and may be brown, maroon, mottled, red, orange, or cream. One of the most popular shells. (Pls. 124, 133.)

25-3 NOBLE SCALLOP, *Chlamys nobilis* Reeve; Western Pacific; 3 to 5 inches; a really choice and beautifully colored species which ranges from dull brown to maroon, red, yellow, orange, or purple. So vivid are the colors that novices frequently believe them to have been artificially dyed. (Pls. 121, 123.)

25-4 DOUGHBOY SCALLOP, *Chlamys asperrimus* Lamarck; southeastern Australia; 3 to 4 inches. Similar to the preceding, but shell thinner and more inflated. Coloration also variable, from brown or purple to solid red or lemon yellow. This is a commercially important species, particularly in Tasmanian waters. (Pl. 123.)

25-5 SWIFT'S SCALLOP, *Chlamys swifti* Bernardi; Japan; 3 to 5 inches; usually shades of pink on the upper valve and the lower one white. In shape, it is reminiscent of the Lion's Paw. Rare color forms occur but are usually in more delicate pastel shades than the brilliant purples and oranges of *Chlamys nobilis*.

25-6 QUEEN SCALLOP, *Chlamys bifrons* Lamarck; southeastern Australia; 3 to 6 inches; an inflated shell, white and lavender markings on the outside but the interior is a deep solid violet. A striking shell in any collection. (Pl. 123)

25-7 ROUGH SCALLOP, *Chlamys muscosus* Wood; Florida and West Indies; about 1 inch. A small and uncommon species with the shell covered with fine raised scales. Coloration very variable, and large series could be assembled, each specimen being differently marked. (Pl. 122.)

25-8 ZIGZAG SCALLOP, *Pecten ziczac* Linné; southeastern United States and West Indies; 2 to 4 inches. Upper valve perfectly flat, lower one arched and commonly white. Another variably marked species, usually red-brown, but may be tan, chocolate, lavender, orange, or white. (Pl. 124.)

25-8a CRUSADER'S SCALLOP, *Pecten jacobeus* Linné; Mediterranean Sea; 3 to 6 inches; upper valve flat, brown to orange; lower valve arched and white. Reputedly worn by those who had been to the Holy Land in the Middle Ages. Later worn by pilgrims to the shrine of Saint James de Compostela in Spain. (Pl. 45.)

THE THORNY OR SPINY OYSTERS
(Family Spondylidae)

These bivalves are not oysters as the vernacular name would imply but are more closely related to the scallops. In life they are usually coated with lime and marine growths. They live

23-6

25-1

24-1

25-3

25-2

25-6

25-4

25-5

25-7

25-8

25-9

25-10

25-11

25-12

25-13

26-1

27-1

28-1

29-1

29-3

29-2

29-4

29-5

attached to dead coral or submerged wood. Specimens are nearly always collected by divers. A few species attain a size of one foot or more and weigh as much as 20 pounds; but these are generally ugly. It is the smaller specimens with long projecting spines and vivid colors that are desired by collectors and decorators.

25-9 MEDITERRANEAN THORNY OYSTER, *Spondylus gaederopus* Linné; Mediterranean Sea; 3 to 5 inches. A shell with the two valves differently colored: upper valve dark violet, purple, or maroon; lower valve pure white. This is the only large species of the family occurring in the Mediterranean Sea. (Pl. 108.)

25-10 PANAMIC THORNY OYSTER, *Spondylus princeps* Broderip; Gulf of California southward along the west coast of Central America; 3 to 5 inches; shell may be red, brick red, white, rose, or a combination of these colors. Spines long and numerous, often spatulate and slightly curved. Formerly *Spondylus pictorum* Schreibers. (Pl. 97.)

25-11 AMERICAN THORNY OYSTER, *Spondylus americanus* Hermann; Florida and Caribbean; 3 to 6 inches. Similar to 25-10, but distinguishable from the Eastern Pacific species by the more oval shape, different coloration, and spines usually straight. White, orange, lavender, pink, and other shades; rarely red. (Pls. 42, 61, 98, 125.)

25-12 LONG-SPINED THORNY OYSTER, *Spondylus wrightianus* Crosse; northern Australia; 3 to 6 inches in diameter; usually white, cream, or rose. Remarkable for its quite small body and greatly produced spines. (Pl. 146.)

25-13 DUCAL THORNY OYSTER, *Spondylus ducalis* Röding; Indo-Pacific; 3 to 5 inches; a rather nondescript species; shell usually dark; may be brown, red-brown, or gray, tan, or other colors. Spines short, very numerous, and white or lighter tinted than the shell. (Pl. 102.)

26. Superfamily Anomiacea

THE JINGLE SHELLS AND SADDLE OYSTERS (Family Anomiidae)

These bivalves belong to a small family of thin, brittle shells with a micalike exterior. Beaches of the eastern United States are often covered with windrows of three-inch shells that jingle when trod upon or kicked, hence the vernacular name, Jingle Shells. In the Philippines quantities of the WINDOW PANE SHELL, *Placuna placenta* Linné, are used as panes to admit light but deflect the rays of the tropic sun.

26-1 SADDLE OYSTER, *Placuna sella* Linné; Indo-Pacific; 4 to 8 inches. A shell similar to the Window Pane Shell in that it starts life as a perfectly flat disk with little space allotted for the inhabitant. As it grows, the shell begins to twist and arch, so that the mature shell closely resembles a saddle. Exterior gray with numerous fragile micalike growth rings; interior dark gray with a high luster. (Pls. 44, 133.)

27. Superfamily Ostreacea

THE TRUE OYSTERS (Family Ostreidae)

Oysters are among the most familiar of all bivalves. The entire body may be consumed (in scallops, only the muscle is eaten). The shells are used in road work and land fill or ground and used as fowl grit. About 50 species are living today.

27-1 COCK'S COMB OYSTER, *Lopha cristagalli* Linné; Indo-Pacific; 3 to 4 inches; exterior strongly ridged, often with erect hollow processes; color red-brown or purplish brown, interior metallic bronze. Found attached to submerged wood and has an affinity for sunken metal wrecks. (Pl. 65.)

Order Eulamellibranchia

28. Superfamily Chamacea

THE JEWEL BOXES (Family Chamidae)

These are somewhat similar to the thorny oysters except that they are usually smaller, averaging between 2 and 3 inches, and have leaf-like foliations. The genus is restricted to the tropics, and there are about 25 species. Many are quite beautiful both in form and coloration.

28-1 LAZARUS' JEWEL BOX, *Chama lazarus* Linné; Indo-Pacific; 4 inches. A very handsome shell, with numerous frondose foliations. Shell may be variously colored, lavender, yellow, rose, white, and other tints. Fairly common. (Pl. 47.)

29. Superfamily Cardiacea

THE COCKLES (Family Cardiidae)

Cockles belong to a large, world-wide family of bivalves, most of which are more or less heart-shaped. Some species are completely smooth, others moderately or heavily ribbed. Some species are spiny or have other ornamentation.

29-1 PRICKLY COCKLE, *Acanthocardia aculeata* Linné; Europe; 3 to 4 inches; light brown, tan, or cream in coloration. Shell with about twenty ribs, each adorned with projecting spines. A favorite with European collectors. (Pl. 148.)

29-2 SMOOTH HEART COCKLE, *Glossus humanus* Linné; Europe; 2½ to 4 inches; shell ivory or tan with brown periostracum. Another favorite; the smooth shell with the spiraled umbo has long been esteemed by collectors, artists, and artisans alike. Better known as *Isocardia cor* Lamarck, a later name. (Pl. 63.)

29-3 ORIENTAL HEART COCKLE, *Glossus vulgaris* Reeve; Western Pacific; 2½ inches; something like a smaller edition of the preceding but with ribbed growth lines and a raised keel along the edge, giving this little shell the true heart shape. Ivory or yellowish. (Pls. 41, 85.)

29-4 BROKEN HEART COCKLE, *Corculum cardissa* Linné; Indo-Pacific; 2 to 3 inches. Another species that has the heart-shaped outline, but the shells are quite compressed. Very variable in shape, sculpture, ornamentation, and color. Many varietal names were proposed in the past. Since the two valves separate in the middle, in the Philippines it is called, perhaps facetiously, the "Broken Heart." Color may be solid yellow, pink, orange, white with red spots, and various other combinations. (Pl. 45.)

THE GIANT CLAMS (Family Tridacnidae)

In this small family of five species are to be found the largest species of shelled mollusks. The GIANT CLAM, *Tridacna gigas* Linné, attains a maximum length of 4 feet and a weight of up to 600 pounds. The huge fleshy mantle extends over the fluted lip of the shell. Colonies of algae are farmed by the clam and serve as a supplemental food supply.

29-5 FLUTED GIANT CLAM, *Tridacna maximus* Röding; Indo-Pacific; 3 to 12 inches; coloration variable, white, yellow, orange, or banded with combinations of these colors. Shell somewhat variable in shape and development of the large fluted scales. (Pls. 46, 64, 103.)

30. Superfamily Veneracea

THE VENUS CLAMS (Family Veneridae)

Venus clams belong to a large family, there being some five hundred species distributed around the world. The familiar HARD-SHELL CLAM, *Mercenaria mercenaria* Linné, of clam chowder or clams on the halfshell is a member of this family. Formerly American Indians cut disks from the purple margin of the shell and fashioned their wampum belts from strings of disks.

30-1 PLICATE VENUS, *Circomphalus plicata* Gmelin; West Africa; 2½ to 3½ inches; shape similar to the familiar Hard Clam, but surface with numerous raised ribs; color tan to purplish brown; interior white. Uncommon. (Pl. 132.)

30-2 PANAMIC COMB VENUS, *Pitar lupinaria* Lesson; west Mexico south to Peru; 1½ to 3 inches. A typical clam shell but with a row of spikelike spines; in smaller individuals their development is usually more spectacular. Shell white with violet tints. (Pl. 149.)

30-3 CHOCOLATE FLAMED VENUS, *Lioconcha castrensis* Linné; Indo-Pacific generally; 2 to 3 inches; shell smooth and of the typical clam shape; surface covered with a number of chocolate zigzag markings; shell cream-colored, interior white. (Pl. 167.)

30-4 ELEGANT DISK CLAM, *Dosinia elegans*

Conrad; Gulf of Mexico; 2 to 3 inches; shell flattened, disklike, with numerous concentric ridges; cream to straw-colored. (Pl. 131.)

30-5 MESHED PAPHIA, *Paphia undulata* Born; Indo-Pacific; 2 to 3 inches; shell elongate, similar to the Sunray Venus from the southeastern United States; ground color cream or yellow with a network of orange or buff-colored lines, interior cream.

30-6 FRILLED VENUS, *Chione gnidia* Broderip and Sowerby; west Mexico south to Peru; 2 to 4 inches; several concentric rows of frilled lamellae; white or beige; white interior. (Pl. 143.)

30-7 WEDDING CAKE VENUS, *Callanaitis disjecta* Perry; southeastern Australia; 2 to 2½ inches; a fantastically sculptured shell, cream to pinkish, with fluted lamellar ridges which are thin and brittle. Rarely found perfect. (Pl. 43.)

31. Superfamily Mactracea

THE SURF CLAMS (Family Mactridae)

Surf clams belong to a family of large, brittle bivalves with a depression in the hinge area. Edible species are commercially important.

31-1 ATLANTIC SURF CLAM, *Spisula solidissima* Dillwyn; east coast of the United States; 4 to 8 inches; a large, unattractive shell, triangular in shape; brownish periostracum on a white shell. One of the commonest American shells.

31-2 RANGIA CLAM, *Rangia cuneata* Gray; southeastern United States; 1 to 2½ inches; periostracum tan, white shell. A common species that occurs in salt marshes along the coast.

32. Superfamily Tellinacea

THE TELLINS (Family Tellinidae)

A large family of more than 200 species. The shells are thin, flattened, usually beautifully colored with pastel tints. The tellins are sand dwellers and active burrowers. The superfamily is widely distributed; most species are tropical.

32-1 ORANGE TELLIN, *Tellina foliacea* Linné; Indian Ocean; 2½ inches; a flattened shell, solid orange or dark honey colored. Not common.

THE DONAX OR WEDGE SHELLS (Family Donacidae)

These belong to a family of clams usually inhabiting the intertidal zone. The BUTTERFLY DONAX, *Donax variabilis* Say, of the southeastern United States, attain a size of only 3/4 inch yet are so abundant that they are often gathered for food; coquina soup is a clear broth made from quantities of them. The shell is one of the most variably marked of any mollusk.

32-2 KEELED DONAX, *Donax scorteum* Linné; Indian Ocean; 3 to 3½ inches, one of the largest species of the family. Shell with concentric rib-

30-1

30-2

30-3

30-4

30-5

30-6

30-7

31-1

31-2

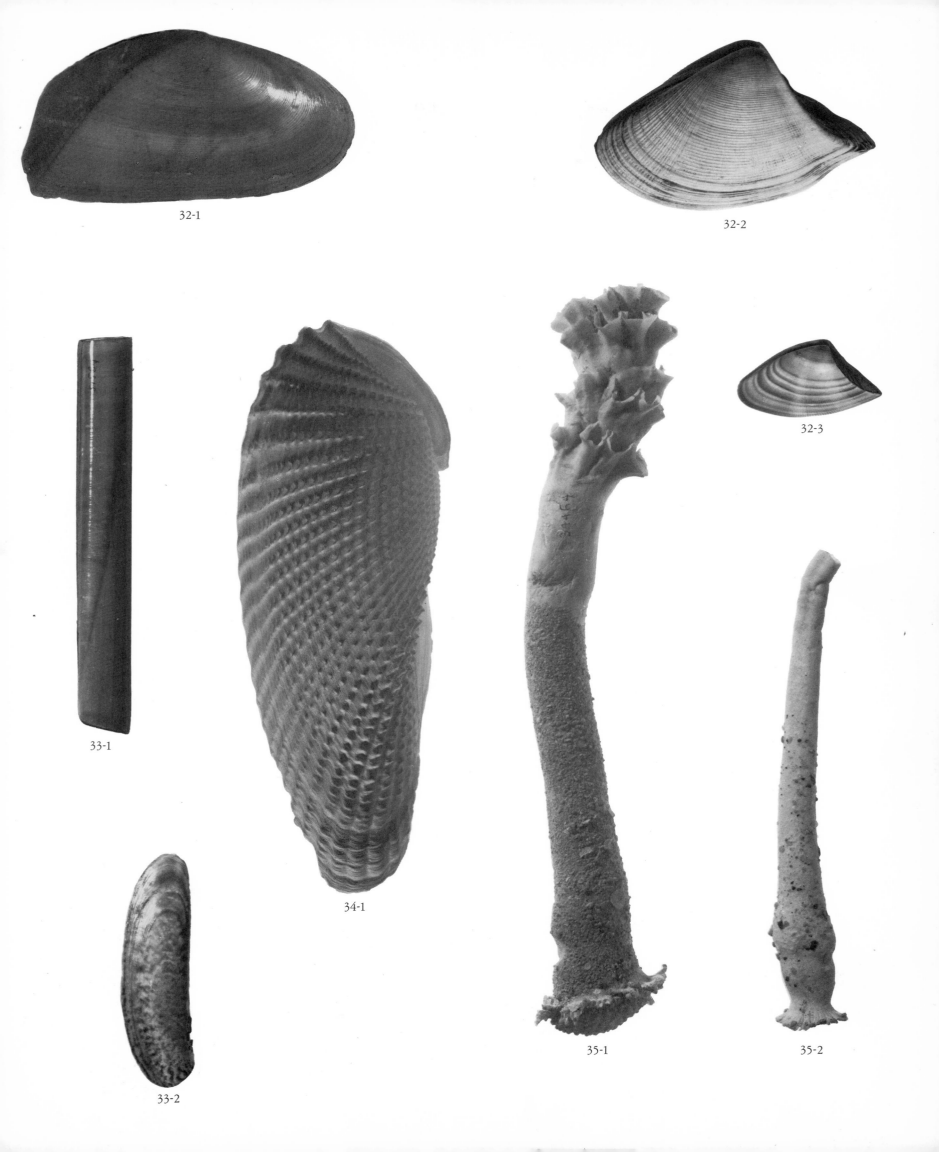

32-1

32-2

32-3

33-1

34-1

35-1

35-2

33-2

bing; juvenile shells with small spines on the ridge of the keel. Color gray with lavender tinting, interior violet stained. Not common.

32-3 CARINATE DONAX, *Donax carinata* Hanley; west Mexico and west coast of Central America; 1 to 1½ inches; similar to the preceding but smaller in size; exterior purplish brown, interior purple. Fairly common.

33. Superfamily Solenacea

THE RAZOR CLAMS (Family Solenidae)

These bivalves possess two thin, elongate shells held together by a small ligament. They are active diggers and burrowers on sandy beaches. About fifty species are known.

33-1 GOULD'S SOLEN, *Solen gouldi* Conrad; Japan and East Asia; 5 inches. In this species the two edges of the shell are exceedingly straight; the valves are slightly arched, the clam being confined to the area within. Shell olivaceous.

THE CULTELLA RAZORS
(Family Cultellidae)

These form a family of clams in which the delicate valves are wider and even more flattened than those of the true razor clams. Many species have a raised rib inside the thin shell for further support. A number of the species, particularly the larger ones, are very good to eat.

33-2 PHILIPPI'S RAZOR, *Phaxas philippianus* Dunker; Western Pacific; 2 to 2½ inches; shell thin, olive and white, mottled with tan blotches.

34. Superfamily Pholadacea

THE PHOLADS OR PIDDOCKS
(Family Pholadidae)

These bivalves are a cosmopolitan family of boring clams. They burrow into mud, peat, wood, or rock. In most species the siphon is large and muscular while the shell is small and gaping. Also placed in this superfamily are the most destructive of mollusks, the shipworms (family Teredinidae), which do millions of dollars of damage annually. In this group, the vestigial shell is further reduced and the animal is long and wormlike. They bore into wooden hulls, pilings, and wharfs, eventually destroying them.

34-1 ANGEL'S WING, *Cyrtopleura costata* Linné, east coast of North America; 4 to 8 inches; one of the loveliest of shells, the familiar Angel's Wing is white with radiating scaled ribs. Live specimens are a dirty gray, and the immaculate cabinet specimens have usually been bleached to remove all traces of stain and discoloration. Better known as *Barnea costata* Linné. (Pl. 40.)

35. Superfamily Clavagellacea

THE WATERING POTS
(Family Clavagellidae)

These bivalves are among the oddest and most unusual of mollusks. Beginning life as a small, ordinary clam, they form a calcareous tube as they mature. The lower end of the tube is perforated, like a watering-pot spout, hence the common name. The upper end, which extends above the substrate, is covered with leafy foliations. Several species from various parts of the Indo-Pacific have been described. Rare.

35-1 WATERING POT, *Penicillus australis* Chenu; Western Pacific; 4 to 8 inches. A typical species; the original tiny pair of valves are barely visible in a notch in the lower left-hand corner of the tube. The tube is covered with sand grains and pebbles. Grayish white in color. (Pl. 33.)

35-2 LESSER WATERING POT, *Penicillus novazelandiae* Bruguière; southwestern Pacific; 3 to 4 inches; a smaller and less ornate species, lacks the foliations on the open end; shell white.

Class Cephalopoda

The cephalopods are a group of highly specialized mollusks possessing well developed eyes and the ability to move rapidly by means of jet propulsion. Most lack an external shell. The subclass Dibranchia contains the squids, octopuses, and cuttlefish. They have eight or ten arms, with rows of suckers, and one pair of gills. The largest living mollusk, the Giant Squid, is placed here. Cuttlebone, fed to caged birds for calcium, is the internal shell of the cuttlefish.

Subclass Tetrabranchia

This subclass is distinguished from the Dibranchia by having numerous small arms lacking suckers and possessing two pairs of gills. There are more than five thousand extinct species of ammonites and their close relatives. The *Nautilus* is the sole surviving representative of the subclass and the only cephalopod retaining an external shell.

36-1 CHAMBERED NAUTILUS, *Nautilus pompilius* Linné; Western Pacific; 5 to 8 inches, with larger and juvenile shells being collector's items. The shell is rather thin and brittle. Coloration is whitish with brown stripes toward the smaller end. The interior is composed of numerous septa or chambers, the soft parts of the animal occupying the outermost. The surface layer is often removed (by the use of acid or sandblasting, rather than buffing) to reveal the nacreous layer. Hence, the other vernacular name, the Pearly Nautilus. (Pls. 82, 112.)

Glossary

Adaptation. The fitness of a structure, function, or entire organism for a particular environment; the evolutionary process of becoming so fitted.

Adaptive. Fitted for a particular environment.

Aestivate. To pass the summer in a quiet, torpid condition.

Anal orifice. The posterior opening of the digestive tract.

Anterior. The forward or head end; opposite of posterior.

Aperture. Opening at the last-formed margin of a gastropod shell through which the head and foot may extend in life.

Apex. The tip of the spire in snail shells.

Apical. At the apex or top.

Aquatic. Pertaining to or living in water.

Aragonite. A mineral composed, like calcite, of calcium carbonate, but differing from calcite in certain characters of crystallization, density, and cleavage.

Auricle. The receiving chamber of the heart.

Axis. A line of reference or one about which parts are arranged symmetrically; the center around which the whorls coil.

Base. The extremity opposite the apex in snail shells.

Bathymetry. The measurement of depths of water in oceans, seas, and lakes.

Beak. The small tip of a bivale shell, near or above the hinge, marking the point where growth of shell started; *see* Umbo.

Bilateral symmetry. Symmetry such that a body or part can be divided by one medial plane into equivalent right and left halves, each a mirror image of the other.

Biota. The flora and fauna of a region.

Bivalve. A clam or other representative of the class Bivalvia; a shell with two valves.

Body whorl. The last formed and largest whorl of a snail shell.

Brackish. Slightly salty; said of water that has a salinity between fresh water and sea water.

Byssus. The threads by which certain bivalves attach their shells or bodies to solid objects.

Calcareous. Composed of or containing calcium carbonate.

Calcite. A mineral, calcium carbonate, crystallized in hexagonal form and thus distinguished from aragonite.

Callus. A growth of shelly material composing a thickened layer, especially around the aperture in gastropods.

Cambrian. The geologic period representing the oldest of the systems into which the Paleozoic rocks are divided.

Canal. A grooved projection of the lip of the aperture in many snail shells.

Carina (pl. *Carinae)*. A keel-like ridge.

Carnivorous. Eating or living on the flesh of other animals.

Cenozoic. An era of geologic time marking the close of the Mesozoic era up to and including the present; including the geologic periods called Tertiary and Quaternary.

Cephalic. Pertaining to or toward the head.

Chitin. A horny, organic substance as in the ligament of bivalves, the operculum of some gastropods, and the internal shell of squids.

Chitinous. Composed of chitin.

Cilium (pl. *Cilia)*. A microscopic hairlike process attached to a free cell surface, often capable of vibration.

Coelenterates. Aquatic animals placed in the phylum Coelenterata, or Cnidaria, including hydroids, jellyfishes, sea anemones, and soft and stony corals.

Columella. The axial pillar around which the whorls of the snail shell coil, commonly visible at inner lip of aperture.

Community. A group of organisms of one or more species living together and related by environmental requirements.

Conchiolin. Material composed of protein of which the periostracum and organic matrix of the limy parts of the shell are composed.

Conchology. The study of molluscan shells; *see also* Malacology.

Conic. Shaped like a cone.

Continental shelf. The shallow and gradually sloping ground from the shore of a continent out to the point, usually no more than 100 fathoms deep, where the slope starts to fall away steeply down to the ocean depths.

Crenulate. Finely notched or delicately corrugated, as on the edge of some bivalve shells or the outer lip of some snail shells.

Cuticle. A thin noncellular external covering of an organism.

Denticles. Small projections resembling teeth, around the margin of the gastropod aperture.

Dextral. Right-handed; coiled in a right-hand spiral, in a clockwise manner; said of snails having the aperture on the right side of the shell when the apex is held upward; opposite of sinistral.

Dioecious. With the male and female organs in separate individuals; separate sexes.

Distal. Away from the point of attachment or place of reference.

Dorsal. Toward or pertaining to the back or upper surface.

Ecological niche. The position of an organism within its community and ecosystem, resulting from its structural adaptations, physiological responses, and specific behavior.

Ecosystem. A natural unit that includes living and nonliving parts interacting to produce a stable system, *e.g.*, a lake.

Environment. The totality of physical, chemical, and biotic conditions surrounding an organism.

Equilateral. With the parts of the bivalve shell anterior and posterior to the beaks equal or nearly equal in length.

Esophagus. That part of the digestive tract between the pharynx and stomach.

Exoskeleton. An external supporting structure or covering.

Fauna. The animal life living in a given region or during a specified period of time.
Flora. The plant life living in a given region or during a specified period of time.
Fossil. Any remains of an organism preserved in the earth or rocks by natural causes in past geological time.

Ganglion (pl. Ganglia). A group or concentration of nerve-cell bodies set apart and acting as a center of nervous influence.
Gastropod. A snail or other representative of the class Gastropoda, comprising primarily univalve shells but also including such shell-less animals as slugs and nudibranchs.
Gill. An organ for aquatic respiration.

Habitat. The place where an organism lives.
Helical. Spirally coiled; following the course of a spiral.
Helicocone. Distally expanding coiled tube that forms most gastropod shells.
Herbivorous. Feeding only or chiefly on vegetable matter.
Hermaphrodite. An animal with both male and female reproductive organs.
Hibernate. To pass the winter in an inactive or torpid condition.
Hinge. Interlocking tooth devices of the valves of bivalve shells.
Homology. Fundamental similarity; structural likeness of an organ or part in one kind of animal with the comparable unit in another resulting from descent from a common ancestry.
Hyperstrophic. Having an apparently sinistral shell with a dextrally organized animal (*ultradextral*), or a seemingly dextral shell with a sinistrally organized animal (*ultrasinistral*); usually detected only from a study of the soft parts.

Incised. Sculptured with depressed lines or grooves.
Inner lip. The portion of aperture near the basal part of the columella.
Integument. An outer covering of an animal.
Invertebrate. Any animal without a dorsal column or vertebrae.

Labial palps. Fleshy flaps located on each side of the esophagus of bivalves that serve to sort food particles.
Lamella (pl. Lamellae). A thin plate.
Ligament. Cartilage and elastic resilium connecting the valves of bivalves at the umbo.
Littoral. Belonging to, inhabiting, or taking place near the seashore.

Malacology. The study of mollusks concerning the soft anatomy as well as the shell.
Mantle. The membrane which encloses the molluscan viscera and secretes the shell and periostracum.

Marine. Pertaining to or inhabiting the sea, ocean, or other saline waters.
Mesozoic. An era of geologic time between the Paleozoic and the Cenozoic eras.
Monoecious. Having both male and female gonads in the same individual; hermaphroditic.
Morphological. Having to do with the structure or form of organisms.

Nacre. Type of shell structure consisting of thin leaves of aragonite lying parallel to the inner surface of the shell, and exhibiting a characteristic luster, commonly iridescent.
Nacreous. Consisting of, or having the character of nacre.
Nephridium. A tubular excretory organ found in mollusks and certain other invertebrates.
Nocturnal. Pertaining to night.

Omnivorous. Feeding on both animal and vegetable substances.
Operculum. The horny or calcareous structure covering the apertural opening of some snail shells.
Oral. Pertaining to or near the mouth.
Ordovician. The second of the geologic periods comprised in the Paleozoic era; the system of strata deposited during that period.
Organ. A group of cells or tissues functioning as a unit for some special purpose.
Outer lip. The outer edge of the aperture of snail shells.

Paleozoic. An era of geologic time between the Precambrian and Mesozoic eras.
Pallial line. The impression or scar on the inner surface of the bivalve shell marking the attachment of the mantle.
Pallial sinus. An indentation in the pallial line.
Parietal wall. Inside wall of shell within the aperture of snails, nearest the columella.
Pelagic. Pertaining to the open ocean.
Pericardium. The cavity enclosing the heart.
Periostracum. The skinlike outer covering of many shells.
Periphery. The edge or boundary of an area.
Pharynx. The region of the digestive tract between the mouth cavity and the esophagus.
Phylogeny. The evolutionary history of a species or a related group of animals.
Phylum. The chief division in the hierachy of classification of the Animal and Plant Kingdoms, *e.g.*, the phylum Mollusca.
Plankton. A term applied to the drifting forms of plant and animal life found in the upper layers of a body of marine or fresh water.
Planospiral. Coiled in a single plane.
Polyp. The individual, asexual member of a hydroid or coral colony, or a sea anemone; commonly attached at the base, but may be free-floating in some species.

Population. A group of individuals belonging to a single species living in a given location.

Porcellaneous. Having a translucent, porcelainlike appearance.

Posterior. The hinder part, or toward the rear end; opposite of anterior.

Predator. An animal that captures or preys upon other animals for its food.

Prismatic. Type of shell structure consisting of prisms of calcite or of aragonite.

Process. A projection.

Prodissoconch. A shell secreted by the larva or embryo and preserved at the beak of some adult bivalves.

Protandric. Referring to a hermaphroditic animal that is first male and later female; some hermaphrodites may alternate sexually several times during their life spans.

Protandry. Production first of sperm and later in life eggs by the same gonad.

Protoconch. The apical whorls of a shell, especially where clearly demarcated from the later whorls.

Radula. The dental apparatus possessed by most snails and all other mollusks except the Bivalvia, composed of a ribbon to which are fixed numerous plates or teeth.

Recent. Of species which still exist; antonym of fossil.

Resilifer. The socketlike structure that supports the internal ligament in certain bivalves.

Resilium. The internal ligament, in a resilifer, under compressed stress.

Retrogression. A reversal in development or condition; passing from a higher to a lower form.

Sessile. Fixed, sedentary, not moving.

Sinistral. Left-handed; coiled in left-hand spiral, in a counterclockwise manner; said of snails having the aperture on the left side of the shell when the apex is held upward; opposite of dextral.

Sinus. A cavity or enlargement as in a blood vessel, or an indentation or deeply cut cavity as in a shell.

Siphon. A tubelike extension of the mantle by which water enters or leaves the mantle cavity.

Spire. The upper whorls, the coils above the body whorl of a snail shell.

Stria (pl. *Striae*). A very fine line.

Substrate. An ecological term denoting the base on which an organism lives, *e.g.*, the sandy bottom of an aquatic environment.

Suture. The junction between whorls of a snail shell.

Symbiosis. Mutually beneficial association of two different species.

Teeth. Dentatelike nodules resembling teeth, as in the aperture of some snails, or in the hinge of most bivalves; also the chitinous plates of the radula.

Temporal. Of or related to time.

Terrestrial. Belonging to or living on the ground.

Tertiary. The earlier of the two geologic periods comprised in the Cenozoic era; the system of strata deposited during that period.

Trifid. Divided more or less equally into three parts or sections.

Tortion. The embryological process in which the body of some gastropods is twisted by rotating the parts of the larval mollusk behind the head 180 degress counterclockwise; independent of the process by which the shell is helically coiled in the form of a helicocone.

Trochophore. A free-swimming ciliate larva typical of marine annelid worms, but occurring in other invertebrate groups, including some of the mollusks.

Ultradextral. Of a shell which appears to be sinistral but has a dextrally organized animal; *hyperstrophic*.

Ultrasinistral. Of a shell which appears to be dextral but has a sinistrally organized animal; *hyperstrophic*.

Umbilicus. A small hollow commonly at the center of the base of the body whorl in some shells.

Umbo (pl. *Umbones*). The earliest part of the bivalve shell as seen from the outside.

Univalve. A snail or other representative of the class Gastropoda having a single shell.

Varix (pl. *Varices*). A prominently raised ventral ridge on the surface of snail shells originally formed at the aperture.

Veliger. A larval mollusk in the stage where it has a ciliated swimming membrane or membranes; the bearer of a velum.

Velum. A thin membranous covering.

Ventral. Toward the lower side or belly; away from the back.

Ventricle. The muscular chamber of the heart which by contraction forces the blood through the vessels.

Vermiform. Resembling a worm in shape.

Viscus (pl. *Viscera*). An internal organ of the body, especially those of the visceral cavity.

Whorl. One complete spiral turn (volution) of the spire as in most snail shells.

Bibliography

Books for the Beginning Student of Mollusks

Dance, S. Peter. SHELL COLLECTING: AN ILLUSTRATED HISTORY. 344 pp., 35 plates. University of California Press, Berkeley. 1966.

–. RARE SHELLS. 128 pp., colored photos. University of California Press, Berkeley and Los Angeles. 1969.

Jacobson, Morris K., and William Emerson. WONDERS OF THE WORLD OF SHELLS: SEA, LAND, AND FRESH WATER. 80 pp., illustrated in black and white. Dodd, Mead and Company, New York. 1971.

Johnstone, Kathleen Y. SEA TREASURE: A GUIDE TO SHELL COLLECTING. 242 pp., 8 color plates, numerous text figures. Houghton Mifflin Co., Boston. 1957.

–. COLLECTING SEASHELLS. 198 pp., illustrated in color and black and white. Grosset & Dunlap, New York. 1970.

Stix, Hugh, Marguerite Stix, and R. Tucker Abbott. THE SHELL: FIVE HUNDRED MILLION YEARS OF INSPIRED DESIGN. 188 pp., illustrated in color and black and white. Harry N. Abrams, Inc., New York. 1968.

General Reference and Identification Books

Abbott, R. Tucker. SEA SHELLS OF THE WORLD. 160 pp., 790 figures in color of 562 of the better-known species. A Golden Nature Guide. Golden Press, New York. Paperback and hardcover. 1962.

Boss, Kenneth J. CRITICAL ESTIMATE OF THE NUMBER OF RECENT MOLLUSCA. OCCASIONAL PAPERS ON MOLLUSKS. Vol. 3, No. 40, pp. 81–136. Museum of Comparative Zoology, Cambridge, Massachusetts. 1971.

Hedgpeth, Joel W., editor. TREATISE ON MARINE ECOLOGY AND PALEOECOLOGY. Vol. 1, Geological Society of America, Memoir 67, VIII + 1296 pp., illustrations. Boulder, Colorado. 1957.

Hyman, Libbie H. THE INVERTEBRATES. Vol. 6, Mollusca I, Aplacophora, Polyplacophora, Monoplacophora, Gastropoda: The Coelomate Bilateria. 792 pp., illustrated. McGraw-Hill, New York. 1967.

Morton, J. E. MOLLUSCA. 244 pp., 41 figures. Hutchinson University Library, London. 1967.

Rogers, Julia E. THE SHELL BOOK. 485 pp., 87 plates (8 in color). Charles T. Branford Co., Boston. Reprint of 1908 edition with the names brought up to date in an appendix by Harald A. Rehder. 1960.

Regional Identification
New World
Marine – Western Atlantic

Abbott, R. Tucker. SEASHELLS OF NORTH AMERICA: A GUIDE TO FIELD IDENTIFICATIONS. 280 pp., illustrated in color. Golden Press, New York. 1968.

Bousfield, E. L. CANADIAN ATLANTIC SHELLS. V + 72 pp. National Museum of Canada, Ottawa. (A handbook of mollusks of northeastern North America; also includes a few other common invertebrates of that region.) 1960.

Clench, William J., et al. JOHNSONIA. Monographs of the Marine Mollusca of the Western Atlantic. Vols. 1–4 already published. Museum of Comparative Zoology, Cambridge, Massachusetts. Numbers issued at intervals. (Excellent figures, descriptions, ranges, collecting localities, book reviews, and so forth.) 1942 to date.

Morris, Percy A. A FIELD GUIDE TO THE SHELLS OF OUR ATLANTIC AND GULF COASTS. Revised ed. 236 pp., 45 plates (8 in color). Houghton Mifflin Co., Boston. 1951.

Warmke, G. L., and R. T. Abbott. CARIBBEAN SEASHELLS. 346 pp., 44 plates (4 in color), text figures and distribution maps. Livingston Publ. Co., Narbeth, Pennsylvania. A guide to the marine mollusks of Puerto Rico and other West Indian islands, Bermuda, and the lower Florida Keys. 1961.

Marine – Eastern Pacific

Keen, A. Myra. SEA SHELLS OF TROPICAL WEST AMERICA: MARINE MOLLUSKS FROM BAJA CALIFORNIA TO PERU. 2nd ed. 1064 pp., 22 color plates, 4,000 figures. Stanford University Press, Stanford, California. 1971.

Morris, Percy A. A FIELD GUIDE TO SHELLS OF THE PACIFIC COAST AND HAWAII, INCLUDING SHELLS OF THE GULF OF CALIFORNIA. Second edition. XXXIII + 297 pp., 72 plates in color and black and white, figures. Peterson Field Guide Series. Houghton Mifflin Co., Boston. 1966.

McLean, James H. MARINE SHELLS OF SOUTHERN CALIFORNIA. 104 pp., 54 plates. Los Angeles County Museum of Natural History, Los Angeles. Science Series 24, Zoology No. 11. 1969.

Old World
Marine – Indo-Pacific, Japan, Australia

Abbott, R. Tucker, et al. INDO-PACIFIC MOLLUSCA. Monographs of the Marine Mollusca of the Indo-Pacific. (East Africa to Polynesia.) Delaware Museum of Natural History, Greenville, Delaware. 1959 to date.

Cernohorsky, Walter O. MARINE SHELLS OF THE PACIFIC. 248 pp., 444 figs. Pacific Publications, Sydney, Australia. 1967.

Habe, Tadashige. SHELLS OF THE WESTERN PACIFIC IN COLOR. Vol. 2, 233 pp. Japan Publications Trading Co., P. O. Box 7752, Rincon Annex, San Francisco. 1964.

Kira, T. SHELLS OF THE WESTERN PACIFIC IN COLOR. 224 pp., 72 color plates. Japan Publications Trading Co., P. O. Box 7752 Rincon Annex, San Francisco. 1962.

Powell, A. W. B. SHELLS OF NEW ZEALAND. 4th ed. 203 pp., illustrations, 36 plates (1 in color), text figures. Whitcombe and Tombs, Ltd., Auckland and London. 1961.

Rippingale, O. H., and D. F. McMichael. QUEENSLAND AND GREAT BARRIER REEF SHELLS. 216 pp., 29 color plates. The Jacaranda Press Pty., Ltd., Brisbane. 1961.

Wilson, Barry R., and Keith Gillett. AUSTRALIAN SHELLS: ILLUSTATING AND DESCRIBING 600 SPECIES OF MARINE GASTROPODS FROM AUSTRALIAN WATERS. 168 pp., 106 pls. in color, 34 text figs. A. H. and A. W. Reed Co., Sydney, and Charles E. Tuttle Co., Rutland, Vermont. 1971.

Marine – West Africa, Europe

Arrecgros, Josette. MUSCHELN AM MEER: SCHNECKEN UND MUSCHELN DER NORDSEE-, ATLANTIK- UND MITTELMEERKÜSTEN. 63 pp., illustrated in color. Verlag Hallwag, Bern. 1958.

Forsyth, W. S. COMMON BRITISH SEA SHELLS. XII + 74 pp., plates and figures. A. and C. Black, Ltd., London. 1961.

Kennelly, D. H. MARINE SHELLS OF SOUTHERN AFRICA. 91 pp., 31 black and white plates. Thomas Nelson and Sons, Johannesburg, South Africa. 1964.

Luther, W., and K. Fiedler. DIE UNTERWASSERFAUNA DER MITTELMEERKÜSTEN. 253 pp., 46 plates (half in color). Mollusca, pp. 163–187, pls. 25–32. Verlag Paul Parey, Hamburg. 1961.

Nickles, Maurice. MOLLUSQUES TESTACES MARINS DE LA COTE OCCIDENTALE D'AFRIQUE. 269 pp., 464 figures. Paul Lechevalier, Paris. 1950.

Nordsieck, Fritz. DIE EUROPÄISCHEN MEERES-GEHÄUSESCHNEKKEN (PROSOBRANCHIA) VOM EISMEER BIS KAPVERDEN UND MITTELMEER. VIII + 273 pp., 31 black and white plates, 4 in color. Gustav Fischer, Stuttgart. 1968.

–. DIE EUROPÄISCHEN MEERESMUSCHELN (BIVALVIA). pp. XIII + 256, 26 black and white plates, 2 in color. Gustav Fischer, Stuttgart. 1969.

Tebble, Norman. BRITISH BIVALVE SEASHELLS: A HANDBOOK FOR IDENTIFICATION. 212 pp., colored and black and white plates. British Museum (Natural History), London. 1966.

World Wide
Marine – Special Groups

Allan, Joyce. COWRY SHELLS OF WORLD SEAS. 170 pp., 15 plates (6 in color). Charles T. Branford Co., Boston. 1960.

Burgess, C. M. THE LIVING COWRIES. 389 pp., illustrated in color and black and white. A. S. Barnes & Co., New York, and Thomas Yoseloff Ltd., London. 1969.

Dees, Lola T. CEPHALOPODS: CUTTLEFISH, OCTOPUSES, SQUIDS. 10 pp., 7 figures. Fishery Leaflet 524. Fish and Wildlife Service, U.S. Department of the Interior, Washington, D.C. 1961.

Lane, Frank W. THE KINGDOM OF THE OCTOPUS: LIFE HISTORY OF THE CEPHALOPODA. 287 pp., 53 plates (5 in color), 13 figures. Sheridan House, New York. 1957.

Laursen, Dan. THE GENUS IANTHINA, A MONOGRAPH. Dana Report, No. 38, 40 pp., 1 pl., 41 figs. Copenhagen. 1953.

Marcy, J., and J. Bot. LES COQUILLAGES: LES GASTÉROPODES MARINS. 281 pp., illustrated in color and black and white. Editions N. Boubée et Cie, Paris. 1969.

Marsh, J. A., and O. H. Rippingdale. CONE SHELLS OF THE WORLD. 166 pp. The Jacaranda Press, Pty., Ltd., Brisbane, Australia. 1964.

Weaver, Clifton S., and John E. duPont. LIVING VOLUTES: A MONOGRAPH OF THE RECENT VOLUTIDAE OF THE WORLD. Monograph Ser. No. 1. 375 plates in color, text figures and maps. Delaware Museum of Natural History, Greenville, Delaware. 1970.

Zeigler, Rowland F., and Humbert C. Porreca. OLIVE SHELLS OF THE WORLD. 96 pp., illustrated in color and black and white. Zeigler and Porreca, West Henrietta, New York. (Distributor: R. E. Petit, Box 133, Ocean Drive Beach, South Carolina 29582.) 1969.

Index

Page citations to the illustrations in the Catalog (pp. 235–282) are not includet in this index.